Social Issues
in Literature

Coming of Age in
William Shakespeare's
Romeo and Juliet

Other Books in the Social Issues in Literature Series:

Social Issues
in Literature

Coming of Age in William Shakespeare's *Romeo and Juliet*

Vernon Elso Johnson, Book Editor

GREENHAVEN PRESS
A part of Gale, Cengage Learning

GALE
CENGAGE Learning™

Detroit • New York • San Francisco • New Haven, Conn • Waterville, Maine • London

GALE
CENGAGE Learning

Christine Nasso, *Publisher*

Elizabeth Des Chenes, *Managing Editor*

© 2009 Greenhaven Press, a part of Gale, Cengage Learning

Gale and Greenhaven Press are registered trademarks used herein under license.

For more information, contact:
Greenhaven Press
27500 Drake Rd.
Farmington Hills, MI 48331-3535
Or you can visit our Internet site at gale.cengage.com

Articles in Greenhaven Press anthologies are often edited for length to meet page requirements. In addition, original titles of these works are changed to clearly present the main thesis and to explicitly indicate the author's opinion. Every effort is made to ensure that Greenhaven Press accurately reflects the original intent of the authors. Every effort has been made to trace the owners of copyrighted material.

Cover image by Hulton Archive/Getty Images.

LIBRARY OF CONGRESS CATALOGING-IN-PUBLICATION DATA

Coming of age in William Shakespeare's Romeo and Juliet / Vernon Elso Johnson, book editor.
    p. cm. -- (Social issues in literature)
    Includes bibliographical references and index.
    ISBN 978-0-7377-4614-3
    ISBN 978-0-7377-4615-0 (pbk.)
    1. Shakespeare, William, 1564-1616. Romeo and Juliet. 2. Maturation (Psychology) in literature. 3. Adolescence in literature. 4. Teenagers in literature. 5. Youth in literature. 6. Parent and child in literature. 7. Adolescence--History. 8. Teenagers--Social conditions. I. Johnson, Vernon E. (Vernon Elso), 1921-
    PR2831.C64 2009
    822.3'3--dc22
                                                      2009009480

Printed in the United States of America
1 2 3 4 5 6 7 13 12 11 10 09

Contents

Chapter 3: Contemporary Perspectives on Coming of Age

Introduction

Romeo and Juliet is one of the most popular and most influential love stories ever written. Why this is true may be as mysterious as love itself, but it surely has something to do with the characters, the verse, and above all, its universal theme of the coming of age of young lovers in a hostile society. Under varied circumstances and with many changes (and once with a happy ending), it has held the stage for more than four hundred years and has seen reincarnations or imitations in all eras. In the twentieth century, it appeared as a ballet by Sergei Prokofiev (1935), a musical by Leonard Bernstein (*West Side Story*, 1957), a show that has been repeatedly revived with great success up to the present time, and in films by Franco Zeffirelli (1968) and Baz Luhrmann (1996). In 2008 alone, more than twenty professional productions were planned around the world.

Around 1595–1596, shortly after London theaters had been closed because of a plague epidemic (1592–1594), Shakespeare produced a new kind of tragedy, a story of doomed young lovers instead of (as in his earlier history plays) the death of kings. The source was a long narrative poem by Arthur Brooke, *The Tragical History of Romeus and Juliet* (1592). Shakespeare followed Brooke's plot closely, but made certain changes for dramatic effect. Central to Shakespeare's play is the idea of very young, true lovers and their coming of age in the midst of a violent feud and a patriarchal culture that brooked no challenge.

One strong influence on the play was a stereotyped pattern of love represented by the Italian poet Petrarch (1304–1374), who wrote hundreds of love-lyrics (sonnets) for a lady, Laura, whom he seemingly never met but for whom he suffered passionately. Petrarch, in turn, was influenced by a medieval cultural phenomenon called courtly love. It was initiated by troubadours in southern France, who, having no social status, sought to achieve some by writing love poems to unreachable (for them) courtly ladies. The convention, or theme, caught on, ultimately influencing the institution of chivalry and the tales of love and adventure that followed. In *Romeo and Juliet*, this theme of love appears as a juvenile phase for Romeo, a step toward growing up, then setting the stage for his meeting Juliet. He walks in the woods at night, weeps, moans for Rosaline, and thinks of nothing but this girl who cares nothing for him, much like Petrarch's lonely suffering for Laura. And if the reader or audience should miss it, Shakespeare has Mercutio remind them: "Now is he in the numbers that Petrarch flowed in."

This pattern of early juvenile love, full of airs and melancholy, results in comedy. The first part of the play is comedic until the deaths of Mercutio and Tybalt. Romeo is sincere and changeless in his almost religious devotion to Rosaline, until he meets Juliet and promptly forgets Rosaline. (Love at first sight was a common belief at the time; that is, invisible arrows shot out from the eyes, two souls met in the air and became soulmates forever.)

Upon meeting Juliet, Romeo forgets his devotion to Rosaline, a mere image of love, and embraces reality in the form of Juliet, although for a brief time he continues to use exaggerated rhetoric before matters turn more serious—and deadly. The lovers are fatally hampered—doomed—by the true villains of the piece: the idiotic older parents who participate in a mindless feud in a stagnant patriarchal system, and a culture of arranged (and enforced) marriages, all of which, in domestic affairs, turn even loving parents into virtual monsters.

Shakespeare changed Brooke's nineteen-year-old Juliet to almost fourteen, an appropriate time for showing complete innocence and ideals plus a newly awakened awareness of true love, in conflict with the sudden interest of Count Paris. Juliet seemingly leaps from childhood to this moment with only her nurse and her parents for companions. Thus, after having accepted and secretly married Romeo, and facing her father's brutal demand that she marry Paris, without considering her preferences, she must make a life or death decision: She can choose Love (with its companion, Death) or Compliance (another marriage that is death to the spirit). She chooses Love. As a result, Juliet faces the task of growing up and its consequences more quickly than does Romeo. She defies her father, the social system, and the feud all at once, refusing to follow the advice of her elders. Like Romeo, she never turns back. Both lovers seem more mature than the careless, purblind parents in this violent society.

Shakespeare was equipped not only with the talent but also with the experience to understand these problems. He was eighteen when he married—too young to marry without the consent of his parents. His father helped him circumvent the usual legal requirements. His bride, Anne Hathaway, daughter of a family friend, was twenty-six and pregnant. Shakespeare produced a family with Anne but then went to work in the London theaters, leaving his family behind. He returned to Stratford in late middle age, leaving Anne his second-best bed. Such details create a problem for scholars as to the nature of the marriage and whether it was arranged.

The following chapters explore the theme of coming of age in *Romeo and Juliet*.

Chapter 1 contains biographical information that is pertinent to the issue at hand. Chapter 2 includes articles on crucial features of maturation in the play: the lovers' extreme youth and rashness, the patriarchal system, the harsh parental control, and the feud itself—all of which fill the air like a deadly fog, driving the lovers to their doom. Chapter 3 discusses the issues in the play that continue today: teenage puppy love, enforced underage marriage, teen suicide, uncertain anguish, loneliness, and violence.

Chronology

1564
William Shakespeare is born at Stratford-upon-Avon.

1570
Shakespeare's father, John, is elected bailiff in Stratford.

1571
Shakespeare probably begins his schooling.

1572
Shakespeare probably witnesses the pageant arranged for Queen Elizabeth's visit to the area.

1576
The Theatre (the first professional theater) opens in the north of London.

1582
William Shakespeare, at eighteen, marries twenty-six-year-old Anne Hathaway.

1583
Five months after their marriage, their daughter Susanna is born.

c. 1585
Shakespeare leaves Stratford to tour with a theater company.

1585
Shakespeare's twins, Hamnet and Judith are born.

1588–1589
Shakespeare goes to London without his family. His first plays are performed.

1590–1592

The Comedy of Errors and three parts of *Henry VI* are presented

1593

Shakespeare writes the tragedy *Titus Andronicus*, which includes the issues of unwanted, arranged marriages, and the comedy *Taming of the Shrew*, about the resolution of an unhappy arranged marriage. Shakespeare acquires a share in the Lord Chamberlain's company. *Richard III* is also staged.

1594

The comedy *Two Gentleman of Verona* is produced—about a father's determination to arrange his daughter's marriage and the elopement that follows.

1595–1596

Five of Shakespeare's plays are produced, including the romantic tragedy *Romeo and Juliet* and the comedies *A Midsummer Night's Dream* and *Love's Labours Lost*. *Richard the II* and *King John* also appear in this period.

1596

Shakespeare's son Hamnet dies.

1597

Shakespeare purchases New Place and other properties in Stratford. *The Merchant of Venice* and *Henry IV, Part I* are produced.

1598

Shakespeare's company moves to the Globe Theatre.

1598–1600

Henry IV, Part II, As You Like It, Much Ado About Nothing, The Merry Wives of Windsor, Henry V, and *Julius Caesar* are presented.

1601

Shakespeare's father dies. *Hamlet* is first performed.

c. 1601–1602

Shakespeare completes *Hamlet*.

1602

Twelfth Night is produced.

1604

Measure for Measure and *Othello* are produced.

1605

King Lear and *Macbeth* are produced.

1606–1608

Shakespeare sees *Pericles, Antony and Cleopatra, Coriolanus, The Winter's Tale*, and *Cymbeline* go into production.

1608

The plague necessitates the closing of playhouses; they remain closed through 1609.

1609

Shakespeare's *Sonnets* are published.

1610

Shakespeare moves back to Stratford. *The Tempest* is staged.

1613

Henry VIII is produced; the Globe Theatre burns down but is rebuilt the following year.

1616

Shakespeare dies.

1623

Anne Hathaway dies. Shakespeare's friends publish thirty-six of his plays, known as the First Folio.

Shakespeare's Background

The Young William Shakespeare

John F. Andrews

John F. Andrews is president of the Shakespeare Guild in Santa Fe, New Mexico, the author of William Shakespeare: His World, Time, and Influence, *and the editor of numerous studies and editions of Shakespeare's works, including* Romeo and Juliet: Critical Essays *(1993).*

In covering the early life of William Shakespeare, John F. Andrews focuses on the social status of Shakespeare's father and the education and coming of age of the playwright, both of which necessitate discussions of Elizabethan marriage. John Shakespeare, William's father, originally a simple farmer, married Mary Arden, his landlord's daughter whose family had greater wealth and social status. After his marriage John came to occupy the highest offices in the city of Stratford. Though William only finished grammar school, his education was excellent. According to Andrews's research, William's marriage at eighteen was "hastily arranged." Anne Hathaway was eight years older, already pregnant, and only had three children by William (unusual at the time). They also lived most of their lives apart, but William remained attached to her as a husband throughout his successes and retirement.

One thing we . . . know is that if Shakespeare was a man for all time, he was also very much a man of his own age. Christened at Holy Trinity Church in Stratford-upon-Avon on 26 April 1564, he grew up as the eldest of five children reared by John Shakespeare, a tradesman who played an

John F. Andrews, "William Shakespeare," in *Dictionary of Literary Biography, vol. 62, Elizabethan Dramatists*, ed. Fredson Bowers, Detroit, MI: Gale Research Company, 1987, pp. 267–353. Copyright © 1987 Gale Research Company. Reproduced by permission of Gale, a part of Cengage Learning.

increasingly active role in the town's civic affairs as his business prospered, and Mary Arden Shakespeare, the daughter of a gentleman farmer from nearby Wilmcote. Whether Shakespeare was born on 23 April, as tradition holds, is not known; but a birth date only a few days prior to the recorded baptism seems eminently probable, particularly in view of the fear his parents must have had that William, like two sisters who had preceded him and one who followed, might die in infancy. By the time young William was old enough to begin attending school, he had a younger brother (Gilbert, born in 1566) and a baby sister (Joan, born in 1569). As he attained his youth, he found himself with two more brothers to help look after (Richard, born in 1574, and Edmund, born in 1580), the younger of whom eventually followed his by-then-prominent eldest brother to London and the theater, where he had a brief career as an actor before his untimely death at twenty-seven.

Marrying for Status

The house where Shakespeare spent his childhood stood adjacent to the wool shop in which his father plied a successful trade as a glover and dealer in leather goods and other commodities. Before moving to Stratford sometime prior to 1552, John Shakespeare had been a farmer in the neighboring village of Snitterfield. Whether he was able to read and write is uncertain. He executed official documents, not with his name, but with a cross signifying his glover's compasses. Some scholars interpret this as a "signature" that might have been considered more "authentic" than a full autograph; others have taken it to be an indication of illiteracy. But even if John Shakespeare was not one of the "learned," he was certainly a man of what a later age would call upward mobility. By marrying Mary Arden, the daughter of his father's landlord, he acquired the benefits of a better social standing and a lucrative inheritance, much of which he invested in property (he bought several houses). And by involving himself in public service, he rose by sure degrees to the highest municipal positions Stratford had to offer: chamberlain (1561), alderman (1565), and bailiff (or mayor) and justice of the peace (1568). A few years after his elevation to the office of bailiff, probably around 1576, John Shakespeare approached the College of Heralds for armorial bearings and the right to call himself a gentleman. Before his application was acted upon, however, his fortunes took a sudden turn for the worse, and it was not until 1596, when his eldest son had attained some status and renewed the petition, that a Shakespeare coat of arms was finally granted. This must have been a comfort to John Shakespeare in his declining years (he died in 1601), because by then he had borrowed money, disposed of property out of necessity, ceased to attend meetings of the town council, become involved in litigation and been assessed fines, and even stopped attending church services, for fear, it was said, "of process for debt." Just what happened to alter John Shakespeare's financial and social position after the mid 1570s is not clear. Some have seen his non-attendance at church as a sign that he had become a recusant, unwilling to conform to the practices of the newly established Church of England (his wife's family had remained loyal to Roman Catholicism despite the fact that the old faith was under vigorous attack in Warwickshire after 1577), but the scant surviving evidence is anything but definitive.

Shakespeare Growing Up

The records we do have suggest that during young William's formative years he enjoyed the advantages that would have accrued to him as the son of one of the most influential citizens of a bustling market town in the fertile Midlands. When he was taken to services at Holy Trinity Church, he would have sat with his family in the front pew, in accordance with his father's civic rank. There he would have heard and felt the words and rhythms of the Bible, the sonorous phrases of the 1559 Book of Common Prayer, the exhortations of the Homilies. In all likelihood, after spending a year or two at a "petty school" to learn the rudiments of reading and writing, he would have proceeded, at the age of seven, to "grammar school." Given his father's social position, young William would have been eligible to attend the King's New School, located above the Guild Hall and adjacent to the Guild Chapel (institutions that would both have been quite familiar to a man with the elder Shakespeare's municipal duties), no more than a five-minute walk from the Shakespeare house on Henley Street. Though no records survive to tell us who attended the Stratford grammar school during this period, we do know that it had well-qualified and comparatively well-paid masters; and, through the painstaking research of such scholars as T.W. Baldwin, we now recognize that a curriculum such as the one offered at the King's New School would have equipped its pupils with what by modern standards would be a rather formidable classical education.

During his many long school days there, young Shakespeare would have become thoroughly grounded in Latin, acquired some background in Greek, and developed enough linguistic facility to pick up whatever he may have wanted later from such modern languages as Italian and French. Along the way he would have become familiar with such authors as Aesop, Caesar, Cicero, Sallust, Livy, Virgil, Horace, Ovid, and Seneca. He would have studied logic and rhetoric as well as grammar, and he would have been taught the principles of composition and oratory from the writings of such masters as Quintilian and Erasmus. In all probability, he would even have received some training in speech and drama through the performance of plays by Plautus and Terence. If Shakespeare's references to schooling and schoolmasters in the plays are a reliable index of how he viewed his own years as a student, we must conclude that the experience was more tedious than pleasurable. But it is difficult to imagine a more suitable mode of instruction for the formation of a Renaissance poet's intellectual and artistic sensibility.

Meanwhile, of course, young Shakespeare would have learned a great deal from merely being alert to all that went on around him. He would have paid attention to the plant and animal life in the local woods that he would later immortalize, in *As You Like It,* as the Forest of Arden. He may have hunted from time to time; one legend, almost certainly apocryphal, has it that he eventually left Stratford because he had been caught poaching deer from the estate of a powerful squire, Sir Thomas Lucy, four miles upstream. He probably learned to swim as a youth, skinny-dipping in the river Avon. He may have participated in some of the athletic pursuits that were the basis of competition in the Elizabethan equivalent of the Olympics, the nearby Cotswold Games. He would undoubtedly have been adept at indoor recreations such as hazard (a popular dice game), or chess, or any of a number of card games. As he grew older, he would have become accustomed to such vocations as farming, sheepherding, tailoring, and shopkeeping. He would have acquired skills such as fishing, gardening, and cooking. And he would have gathered information about the various professions; law, medicine, religion, and teaching. Judging from the astonishing range of daily life and human endeavor reflected in his poems and plays, we can only infer that Shakespeare was both a voracious reader and a keen observer, the sort of polymath Henry James might have been describing when he referred to a character in one of his novels as "a man on whom nothing was lost."

A Hastily Arranged Marriage

Once his school years ended, Shakespeare married, at eighteen, a woman who was eight years his senior. We know that Anne Hathaway was pregnant when the marriage license was issued by the Bishop of Worcester on 27 November 1582, because a daughter, Susanna, was baptized in Holy Trinity six months later on 26 May 1583. We have good reason to believe that the marriage was hastily arranged: there was only one

William Shakespeare (1564-1616). AP Images.

reading of the banns (a church announcement preceding a wedding that allowed time for any legal impediments against it to be brought forward before the ceremony took place), an indication of unusual haste. But whether the marriage was in any way "forced" is impossible to determine. Some biographers (most notably Anthony Burgess) have made much of an apparent clerical error whereby the bride's name was entered as Anne Whateley of Temple Grafton in the Worcester court records; these writers speculate that Shakespeare was originally planning to marry another Anne until Anne Hathaway of Shottery (a village a mile or so from Shakespeare's home in Stratford) produced her embarrassing evidence of a prior claim. To most scholars, including our foremost authority on Shakespeare's life, S. Schoenbaum, this explanation of the Anne Whateley court entry seems farfetched. Such hypotheses are inevitable, however, in the absence of fuller information about the married life of William and Anne Hathaway Shakespeare.

Shakespeare's Love Life

What we do have to go on is certainly compatible with the suspicion that William and Anne were somewhat less than ardent lovers. They had only two more children—the twins, Hamnet and Judith, baptized on 2 February 1585—and they lived more than a hundred miles apart, so far as we can tell, for the better part of the twenty-year period during which Shakespeare was employed in the London theater. If we can give any credence to an amusing anecdote recorded in the 1602–1603 diary of a law student named John Manningham, there was at least one occasion during those years when Shakespeare, overhearing the actor Richard Burbage make an assignation, "went before, was entertained, and at his game before Burbage came; then, message being brought that Richard the Third was at the door, Shakespeare caused return to be made that William the Conqueror was before Richard the Third." If we read the sonnets as in any way autobiographical, moreover, we are shown a poet with at least one other significant liaison: a "Dark Lady" to whom Will's lust impels him despite the self-disgust the affair arouses in him (and despite her infidelity with the fair "Young Man" to whom many of the poems are addressed and for whom the poet reserves his deepest feelings).

But even if there is reason to speculate that Shakespeare may not have always been faithful to the marriage bed, there is much to suggest that he remained attached to Anne as a husband. In 1597 he purchased one of the most imposing houses in Stratford—New Place, across the street from the Guild Chapel—presumably settling his wife and children there as soon as the title to the property was clear. He himself retired to that Stratford home, so far as we can determine, sometime between 1611 and 1613. And of course he remembered Anne in his will, bequeathing her the notorious "second-best bed"—which most modern biographers regard as a generous afterthought (since a third of his estate would have gone to the wife by law even if her name never occurred in the document) rather than the slight that earlier interpreters had read into the phrasing.

Marriage and Money

Peter Holland

Peter Holland is McMeel Family Professor of Shakespeare Studies and acting chair of graduate studies at University of Notre Dame. An international scholar, he is editor of Shakespeare, Memory, and Performance.

The following selection covers circumstances surrounding Shakespeare's marriage to Anne Hathaway, the relationship between his father and Anne's father, Richard Hathaway, and Shakespeare's involvement (in 1612) in a legal suit concerning an unpaid dowry. The Shakespeare family was well known to the Hathaways before William and Anne's marriage, for William's father, John Shakespeare, had acted as surety for Richard Hathaway and had even paid his debts on two occasions. Finally, Holland notes the legal case of an unpaid dowry in which Shakespeare testified, demonstrating that the playwright was "caught up in the kind of arguments over money and marriage that figured in many plays of the period."

• • • by 1582 he was certainly back in Stratford. On 27 November a marriage licence was issued for Shakespeare's marriage to Anne Hathaway (1555/6–1623) (though the record in the bishop of Worcester's register mistakenly refers to the bride as Anne Whateley of Temple Grafton) and on the following day a bond was issued binding Fulke Sandells and John Richardson for the sum of £40 as surety for the marriage, a necessary step since William was at eighteen still a minor and needed his father's consent to the match. Sandells and Richardson had both in 1581 been named

Peter Holland, "Shakespeare, William (1564–1616)," in *Oxford Dictionary of National Biography: In Association with The British Academy: From the Earliest Times to the Year 2000*, ed. H.C.G. Matthew and Brian Harrison, vol. 49, Oxford: Oxford University Press, 2004, pp. 939–976. Copyright © 2004 Oxford University Press. Reproduced by permission of Oxford University Press.

in the will of Richard Hathaway, Anne's father, a yeoman farmer of Shottery, a village just outside Stratford; the will left Anne 10 marks, to be paid when she married.

Anne (whose name also appears as Agnes) was the eldest of Richard's seven children (three with his first wife and four with his second); William may have been a minor, distinctly young for marriage at this time, but Anne was of a normal marrying age. The Shakespeares and Hathaways knew each other: John Shakespeare had acted as surety for Richard Hathaway and twice paid his debts. Whatever the nature of William's relationship with Anne may have been—and biographers and novelists have frequently speculated about it—by the end of summer 1582 Anne was pregnant and the marriage in November was performed after only a single reading of the banns, rather than the more normal three, presumably in order to speed up the process. The vicar who officiated at Temple Grafton, if that was indeed where they married, was John Frith, known for his ability to cure hawks but also 'Unsound in religion', according to a survey in 1586 of the Warwickshire clergy, again a possible indication of Shakespeare's Catholicism. . . .

It is reasonable to give in to temptation and assign Shakespeare's Sonnet 145 to this period, making it Shakespeare's earliest extant work: its final couplet puns on Hathaway ("'I hate" from hate away she threw, / And saved my life, saying "not you."' Sonnet 145, ll. 13–14) and its octosyllabics, unusual in the sonnets, suggest that it may not have been part of the sequence originally. There is no especial reason why a man should write a love poem to a woman only at the beginning of their relationship and the poem need not relate to any actual moment in the history of William and Anne. But, if it were written at the time of the event it appears to describe, then its description of courtship rather than marriage would date it to the early 1580s.

Six months after the marriage, on 26 May 1583, Susanna Shakespeare was baptized, followed on 2 February 1585 by William's and Anne's twins, Hamnet and Judith, probably named after Hamnet and Judith Sadler. Hamnet Sadler, a local baker, was in 1616 one of the witnesses of Shakespeare's will, and his name also appears in local records as Hamlet. With these three children Shakespeare's family seems to have been complete: there are no records of further children. Some have used this as evidence that the marriage was distant or unhappy, though many happily married couples both then and later have had no children at all and it is perhaps relevant that Susanna and Judith had few children (one and three respectively).

The "Lost Years"

From 1585 to 1592 the records of Shakespeare's life are almost silent. He is briefly referred to in records concerning the attempts of his parents to retrieve property in Wilmcote, part of what had been Mary's inheritance and should have been passed on to William, land that had been mortgaged and was now lost, another indication of John's financial troubles. But the reference does not indicate his presence in Stratford. Biographers have created fanciful narratives for this period: none have any foundation. Perhaps this was when he was 'a Schoolmaster in the Countrey'. The traditional explanation, first set out by Nicholas Rowe in his biographical sketch prefixed to his 1709 edition of Shakespeare's plays, was that William poached deer from Sir Thomas Lucy's estate at Charlecote, was caught and prosecuted, wrote a ballad against Lucy, and was forced to escape to London to avoid further prosecution. Shakespeare's apparent jibe at the Lucy coat of arms in *The Merry Wives of Windsor* (I.i, ll. 13–20) has been explained as belated revenge, though why Shakespeare waited so long and revenged himself so obscurely is not adequately justified. . . .

Friends and Lodgings

Records of Shakespeare's friends and family provide other suggestions for his life at this time. Augustine Phillips, a fellow sharer in the King's Men, died in 1604, leaving 'my ffellowe william Shakespeare a Thirty shillings peece in gould' . . . , as he did to other players but naming Shakespeare first. It is reasonable to assume that his fellows in the theatre company were among his closest friends. William Barksted, a minor playwright, wrote warmly of Shakespeare as 'so deere lov'd a neighbor'. . . . Perhaps to this period too belong the stories, anecdotal but not contradicted by the evidence of surviving comments, of his close friendship and genial rivalry with Jonson.

As becomes apparent from the records of a case in 1612, Shakespeare was living from 1602 to 1604 as a lodger with Christopher Mountjoy and his family in Silver Street in the respectable neighbourhood of Cripplegate. The case provides rare glimpses of Shakespeare's London life in 1602–4 and in 1612. Mountjoy, a French Huguenot refugee, with his wife and daughter, was a successful tiremaker who made wigs and head-dresses; Shakespeare might have met them through the French wife of the printer Richard Field who lived nearby but theatre companies always needed the services of wigmakers and the Lord Chamberlain's Men may have been the connection. Other dramatists lived near, including Jonson, Dekker, Munday, and Field, while John Heminges and Henry Condell, fellow sharers, were pillars of a local church, St Mary Aldermanbury.

The case of 1612 was brought by Stephen Belott, Mountjoy's former apprentice, who had married Mountjoy's daughter in 1604 and claimed that Mountjoy had failed to pay the dowry promised. Shakespeare was called as a witness and is mentioned by other witnesses. He helped in the marriage negotiations: Mountjoy asked him to encourage Belott to agree to the match and the young couple made their troth-plight in his presence. . . .

Shakespeare was one of three witnesses examined on 11 May 1612. His deposition brings the closest record of Shakespeare speaking, albeit through the court style of the examiner's clerk. Shakespeare attested that Belott was, in his view. 'A very good and industrious servant' who 'did well and honestly behave himselfe', though he also said that Mountjoy had not 'confesse[d] that he hath gott any great proffitt and comodytye' from Belott's service. He also deposed that the Mountjoys showed Belott 'great good will and affecceon' and that Mrs Mountjoy 'did sollicitt and entreat [him] to move and perswade [Belott] to effect the said marriage and accordingly [he] did'. On the matter of money Shakespeare could not remember (or chose not to remember) how large the marriage portion was to have been, nor whether there was to have been a sum in Mountjoy's will, nor 'what Implementes and necessaries of houshold stuffe' Mountjoy gave Belott as part of the marriage settlement. . . . Further witnesses were examined on 19 June but Shakespeare, though named in the margin of the interrogatories, did not depose again.

In the event the matter was referred to the elders of the French church, who ordered Mountjoy to pay Belott 20 nobles; but Mountjoy, who had fathered two bastards and was excommunicated for his dissolute life, never paid. Whatever the neighbourhood may have been, the Mountjoys were hardly the respectable family they might at first have appeared. The case is trivial enough but it shows Shakespeare caught up in the kind of arguments over money and marriage that figured in many plays of the period.

A Marriage Based on Love?

Peter Ackroyd

Peter Ackroyd, a prolific and eminent English biographer and novelist, is the chief book reviewer for the Times of London. *His latest book is* Thames *(2007).*

In the following article, Peter Ackroyd describes relationships between the families of John Shakespeare and Richard Hathaway (the father of Anne), the circumstances surrounding the courtship and marriage of William and Anne, details of the marriage itself, and customs regarding the conduct expected of officially engaged couples. For example, it was customary for a "troth-plight," which was performed with prescribed ceremonies and the exchange of gifts, to be regarded as binding by society. The two families were well known to each other and had been acquaintances at least since William's childhood, for in 1568 John Shakespeare had paid off some of Richard Hathaway's debts. The Hathaways subsequently became prosperous farmers. Ackroyd also suggests that Shakespeare's sonnet #145 might well have been written for Anne. In general, Ackroyd presents evidence to defend William and Anne from the so-called scandal of what has often been labeled a forced marriage.

In *As You Like It*, the servant Adam suggests that "At seventeen yeeres, many their fortunes seeke". Shakespeare may have sought his fortune among the Lancastrian families of Hoghton Tower and Rufford Hall, but he had returned to his native town. If he there set to work in a lawyer's office, he had at least one consolatory prospect: Anne Hathaway was already well known to him. Fourteen years previously, John Shakespeare had paid off some of her father's debts. The Hathaways were in any case long established in the region. They had been resident in the hamlet of Shottery, at Hewland Farm, since the end of the fifteenth century. Shottery was a mile outside Stratford itself, an area of scattered farms and homesteads on the edge of the Forest of Arden. Anne's grandfather, John Hathaway, was classified as a yeoman and archer; he was esteemed highly enough to have become one of the "Twelve Men of Old Stratford" whod presided at the Great Leet or criminal court. Anne's father, Richard Hathaway, had inherited from him the farm and the property that in subsequent years became known as "Anne Hathaway's Cottage."

A Sensible Arrangement

Richard Hathaway was also a farmer and substantial householder. By his first wife, who came from Temple Grafton, he had three children one of whom was Anne herself. He married again, and had further children. He was eventually "honestly buried" in the manner of the reformed faith, but had named a prominent recusant as an executor of his will; so the religious affiliations of the family, like those of so many other households in the neighbourhood, may have been mixed and ambiguous.

Anne Hathaway was the eldest daughter of the house and as such incurred a fair number of household duties, chief among them the care of her younger siblings. As the daughter of a farming family, too, she learned how to bake bread, to salt meat, to churn butter and to brew ale. In the yard outside the house were poultry and cows, pigs and horses to be fed and reared. Far from being a *mésalliance* or forced marriage, as some have suggested, the partnership of William Shakespeare and Anne Hathaway could have been an eminently sensible arrangement. He may even have exercised a good deal of caution, or common sense, in his choice of a lifelong partner. This was thoroughly in keeping with his practical and business-like approach to all the affairs of the world.

Anne's Age and Education

She was eight years his senior—in the year of their marriage he was eighteen and she was twenty-six—but, in a period of shorter life expectancy, the disparity in age would have seemed greater then than now. It was an unusual arrangement, since in the sixteenth century it was customary for the man to marry a younger woman. The difference in age has of course aroused much speculation, primarily concerned with the wiles of an older female in coaxing an inexperienced young man into bed and eventual marriage. Yet it might, on the contrary, suggest sexual self-confidence on Shakespeare's part. In any case the suspicion does less than justice to Shakespeare's judgement and intelligence which, even at the age of eighteen, might have been acute. It is also an insult to Anne Hathaway who, like many of the silent wives of famous men, has endured much obloquy. Those biographers who enjoy dramatic speculation, for example, have noted that Shakespeare's history plays harbour many manipulative older women, whose beauty seems mysteriously to wither on the vine. In *A Midsummer Night's Dream* Hermia cries out, "O spight! too olde to be ingag'd to young" and the Duke in *Twelfth Night* offers some advice—"Let still the woman take / An elder then her selfe"—and goes on to caution:

Then let thy Love be yonger then thy selfe,

Or thy affection cannot hold the bent;

For women are as Roses, whose faire flowre

Being once displaid, doth fall that verie howre.

But it is probably best to refrain from maladroit interpretation. In the Duke, Shakespeare has created a notorious sentimentalist. It could just as well be argued that, because the females in Shakespeare's drama are literate, so must have been the women around him.

It is not known whether Anne Hathaway could read or write. There was no real opportunity which would have enabled her to learn how to do so and, in any case, 90 per cent of the female population of England were illiterate at that time. It has often been supposed that Shakespeare's two daughters were also illiterate, and so we are faced with the irony of the greatest dramatist in the history of the world surrounded by women who could not read a word he wrote.

There is a sonnet placed as the 145th in Shakespeare's sonnet sequence, which seems oddly situated and out of context. The last two lines suggest that it was in fact composed for Anne Hathaway and has some claim to being the first extant work of William Shakespeare—

"I hate" from "hate" away she threw,

And saved my life, saying "not you."

Hate away is equal to Hathaway. The entire poem is a conventional and youthful paean to a kind and loving mistress, with "lips that Loves owne hand did make.". . .

True Love?

It is to be hoped that "Loves owne hand" had something to do with the match, since Anne Hathaway was four months pregnant by the time of their marriage day. It was not unusual in this period for couples to cohabit before their wedding. Their Stratford neighbours, George Badger and Alice Court, Robert Young and Margery Field, had a similar arrangement. It was also customary for both parties to make a "troth-plight," a verbal contract of marriage before witnesses which was also known as "hand-fasting" or "making sure." So Alice Shaw of Warwickshire declared to William Holder, of the same county, that "I do confesse that I am your wief and have forsaken all my frendes for your sake and I hope you will use me well." The man took the woman's hand, and repeated the same

Anne Hathaway's cottage, Stratford-upon-Avon. Picture Collection, The Branch Libraries, The New York Public Library.

pledge. Only after such a "troth-plight" could the woman give up her virginity. The marriage ceremony came later. It was a code of honour, marked out by both social and sexual discipline; there were of course different forms of "making sure," varying from a private pledge to a ceremony with a prayer book. But its ubiquity can be measured in the fact that between 20 and 30 per cent of all brides bore children within the first eight months of marriage. . . .

The first child of William Shakespeare and Anne Hathaway was probably conceived in the last two weeks of September, for at the end of November the young man or Anne Hathaway's guardians hastened to Worcester in order to obtain a special marriage licence. Anne Hathaway had been left £6 13s 4d by her father, equivalent to a blacksmith's or a butcher's annual wage and enough for her dowry. The licence permitted marriage after a single publication of the banns, and did not specify any particular parish in which the ceremony must take place. The haste was necessary since the period of Advent was at hand, in which marriages were very largely restricted. Another period of prohibition began on 27 January and lasted until 7 April. It was possible, then, that their child might be born when its parents were not formally wedded. Anne's interesting condition may have become evident, and neither she nor her guardians may have wished her child to be illegitimate. . . .

The Wedding

The couple were then invited into the church, where they knelt together in order to partake in the nuptial Mass and blessing; they wore linen cloths or "care cloth" upon their heads to protect them from demons. It was also customary for the bride to carry a knife or dagger suspended from her girdle, the reasons for which are uncertain. (Juliet possesses a dagger, with which she stabs herself.) The bride's hair was unbraided, hanging loose about her shoulders. After the Mass it was customary for a festive procession to return from the church to the house where a wedding feast, or "bride-ale," was prepared. The newly joined couple might then receive gifts of silver, or money, or food. The guests were in turn often given presents of gloves—since Shakespeare's father was a glove-maker, there was no great difficulty in procurement. So we leave them on this apparently auspicious day.

Social Issues
in Literature

CHAPTER 2

Coming of Age in
Romeo and Juliet

Sensing the Doom
of Growing Up

Dympna Callaghan

In her roles as writer and Dean's Professor of Humanities at Syracuse University, Dympna Callaghan does feminist readings of Shakespeare.

Dympna Callaghan interprets what is generally regarded as a story of ideal love in the context of an opposing established culture. Romeo's early love for Rosaline is in the romantic tradition of love, Callaghan notes, involving the unattainable female ideal and the tormented young man. Romeo and Juliet's love-at-first-sight relationship, on the other hand, is in the Platonic convention of finding one's other half. It develops through the accepted stages of first sight, first date, first kiss, engagement, and marriage. But as Juliet senses from the start, the two lovers are, nevertheless, in tragic conflict with family, society, tradition, and economic forces that are resistant to change—a situation that will inevitably result in doom. The play begins in social conflict, develops the romantic theme at its core, and closes with a political ending that gives the promise of change in an older, heretofore stagnant world.

R omeo and Juliet is both the preeminent document of love in the West and the most insistently and exquisitely lyrical of Shakespeare's plays. For precisely this reason, it is tempting to read the play as evidence of the capacity of love and Shakespeare to transcend time rather than as a work immersed in the dominant rhetorical and lyrical tropes of the 1590s. To suggest that this literary rendition of love is a product of its own historical moment denies neither its enduring appeal nor

Dympna Callaghan, "Introduction," in *William Shakespeare: "Romeo and Juliet": Texts and Contexts*, New York: Bedford/St. Martin's, 2003, pp. 1–35. Copyright © 2003 by Bedford/St. Martin's. All rights reserved. Reproduced by permission.

its capacity to speak powerfully to us today. For *Romeo and Juliet* addresses us more fully and more meaningfully in the present when we see the degree to which it is embedded in the past—the present of the 1590s. That is, the play is both of its time and of ours. . . .

Falling in Love

Falling in love is a powerful experience, the description and consequences of which it is the special task of literature to extrapolate. More than anything else, literature takes as its subject matter erotic love, particularly at its most heightened moments, namely those at the beginning of a relationship and during courtship leading up to marriage. . . .

Romeo and Juliet's relationship, then, stands as a cultural ideal that shapes our social understanding about what love should be. Since none of us hopes, consciously at least, for a bloody and tragic conclusion to our erotic relationships, why, we might ask, is *Romeo and Juliet* held up as the consummate ideal? Why do we believe that their love, which is ultimately suicidal after all, is both "natural" and perfect? The point of such questions is not that we should be more cynical. Rather, the point is to help us recognize that our received ideas about *Romeo and Juliet* can sometimes impede our understanding of the text itself. . . .

Although we probably feel that we are at our most authentic when we fall in love, it may well be that we are at our most conventional, following social scripts and codes of which we are almost totally unaware. From "crush" (love at first sight) to full-scale infatuation, to the allegedly "mature" love that is less driven by burning psycho-sexual desperation to possess the beloved, we are almost living a literary genre. We feel compelled to arrive at the socially appropriate "next stage," however that is defined (the date, the kiss, the engagement). . . .

The convention of love at first sight is so compelling in part because it draws upon a perceived truth about the nature

Juliet sensing doom at Romeo's death. Paramount/The Kobal Collection/The Picture Desk, Inc.

of desire. In the *Symposium*, the Greek philosopher Plato (428–327 B.C.E.), tells Aristophanes' story that all human beings were once quadrupeds, male and female conjoined in one creature, who were split in half when they incurred the wrath of the gods. From that time on humans were destined to search and long for the lost part of themselves. . . .

Love and Doom

If we hope to find the self we lost, paradoxically in the very same moment we recognize it outside ourselves, we are, . . . doomed to failure. In the play, this occurs at the most literal level when Romeo and Juliet discover that they have fallen in love with their enemies. Romeo's shocked interrogative "Is she a Capulet?" bespeaks his horror on discovering his mistake: "O dear account! My life is my foe's debt" (1.5.114–15). Similarly, upon discovering that the man she has just fallen in love with is "Romeo, and a Montague, / The only son of your great enemy" (1.5.133–34), Juliet declares:

> My only love sprung from my only hate!
>
> Too early seen unknown, and known too late!
>
> Prodigious birth of love it is to me
>
> That I must love a loathèd enemy. (1.5.135–38).

Here Juliet metaphorically envisages the ominous progeny of this new love, which results from the coupling of incompatible entities, namely love and hate. . . .

Juliet sees early on in the play that this love is doomed from its moment of conception, and while this is a response to the very specific position of the lovers as the son and daughter of feuding parents, there is a level at which hers is an archetypal recognition. After all, is love ever what we thought it would be when we fall in love at first sight? And would it be a good thing if it were?. . .

Romeo's First Love

What happens after love at first sight is, ideally, a love more consciously chosen than the unconscious rapture of romantic passion. When Friar Laurence discovers that Romeo has given over his love of Rosaline for Juliet, he quips: "Young men's love then lies / Not truly in their hearts, but in their eyes" (2.3.67–68). What are we to make, indeed, of Romeo's abrupt change of love object from one woman to another? Benvolio urges him to go to the Capulet feast and "with unattainted eye" (1.2.85) compare Rosaline's beauty with those of the other young women of Verona, and Romeo swears that he will be true to his first love. . . .

Several of the predominant characteristics of eros (sexual love) are worth emphasizing, partly because they are so familiar to us that they have become almost invisible. First, falling in love is a specifically erotic experience—we do not "fall in love" with our parents or with our children. In fact, falling in love typically constitutes a compulsion to move *beyond*, . . . movement outward from our experience of the familiar, the infant "self" or proto-self, to the image beyond. Typically, in erotic love, we move outside our kin, clan, and immediate blood relatives in order make a connection with someone beyond this circle. . . .

Romeo and Juliet, as we have noted, presents an exacerbated friction between the literary and the social, that is, between amatory eloquence and the familial, governmental, economic, and other forces that nonetheless shape and condition it. . . .

Young lovers in the 1590s who saw Shakespeare's play may have left the theater with new expectations about love, which may in turn have provided fresh ammunition in the battle with parents over the choice of a spouse.

Before we first see Romeo, he is described to the audience as the stereotypically languishing lover and the description itself is rendered in idealized, poetic language. The love of Romeo for Rosaline is the embodiment of the Petrarchan cliché, full of exaggerated and empty poetic rhetoric with all the ingredients of grand infatuation. Little wonder that critics have remarked that in terms of psychological representation, Romeo is less mature than Juliet, as we see from Benvolio's description of this romantic anguish:

BENVOLIO: an hour before the worshiped sun

Peered forth the golden window of the east,

A troubled mind drave me to walk abroad,

Where, underneath the grove of sycamore

That westward rooteth from this city's side,

So early walking did I see your son.

Towards him I made, but he was ware of me

And stole into the covert of the wood.

I, measuring his affections by my own,

Which then most sought where most might not be found,

Being one too many by my weary self,

Pursued my humor, not pursuing his,

And gladly shunned who gladly fled from me.

MONTAGUE: Many a morning hath he there been seen,

With tears augmenting the fresh morning's dew,

Adding to clouds more clouds with his deep sighs; (1.1.105–20)

Romeo and Benvolio here follow Petrarch, who succeeded in wallowing in melancholic resignation and in nursing the sting of rejection for more than thirty years. Petrarchanism as a literary form is ostensibly dedicated to extolling female beauty, but in fact uses that beauty as an excuse for exalting a densely aestheticized, tormented masculinity. . . .

During the course of the play, events move from the social, represented by the prose speeches of the Capulet servants Samson and Gregory, to the romantic, represented by the play's extraordinary lyricism. At the end of the play, we are returned to the political world of Veronese society. The final movement is in part a return to the prosaic doggerel of the metrically flatfooted "For never was a story of more woe / Than this of Juliet and her Romeo" (5.3.309–10). But this is also in part a sacred transformation, known in Greek as *metanoia*, change of heart, a moment when ancient enmity becomes present love. We are no longer in the realm of lyricism and romantic love but in that of civic accord, the social bonds of amity that are underpinned by the innate capacity of eros to propel and extend itself from the lover to the beloved, and from the lovers to the wider social order.

Growing Up in
a Violent World

Marjorie Garber

Marjorie Garber is the William R. Kenan Jr. Professor of English and American Literature and a professor of visual and environmental studies at Harvard. Her latest book is Profiling Shakespeare *(2004).*

In the following essay, Marjorie Garber recognizes the enduring appeal of the story of star-crossed lovers, with dynamic supporting characters like Mercutio and the Nurse. The turning point is the death of Mercutio, which, along with Tybalt's death immediately following, changes the play suddenly from comedy to tragedy and affects the entire population of Verona. The design shows Romeo growing from shallowness to maturity and, more impressively, Juliet growing from dependent child to mature woman, as she finds herself increasingly alone, supported only by her love for Romeo. The play is marked from the first by the use of sonnets, telling of civil war and young lovers in a society that pits the very young against the old and powerful, making an integral association of love and death and youth and old age.

Romeo and Juliet, long celebrated as one of the world's great love stories, is also one of Shakespeare's liveliest and most appealing plays. Its tragic tale of "star-crossed lovers" is set against a vivid background of civil strife and domestic controversy in the Italian city of Verona, and its cast includes at least two characters—Juliet's Nurse and Mercutio—who threaten to steal the show. The Nurse, at once bawdy and sen-

Marjorie Garber, *"Romeo and Juliet*: Patterns and Paradigms," in *"Romeo and Juliet"*: *Critical Essays*, ed. John F. Andrews, Danvers, MA: Garland Publishing, Inc., 1993, pp. 119–131. Copyright © 1993 John F. Andrews. All rights reserved. Republished with permission of Taylor & Francis Company, conveyed through Copyright Clearance Center, Inc.

timental, earthy of tongue and soft of heart, has an immediacy about her that cuts across the ages; she is modern and timeless. As for Mercutio, tradition tells us that Shakespeare felt obliged to kill him off in the third act, so that his play would not be usurped—or upstaged—by his own dramatic character. One of Shakespeare's early editors, the poet and critic Samuel Johnson, wrote that "Mercutio's wit, gaiety and courage, will always procure him friends that wish him a longer life," and generations of audiences have borne this out.

Tragedy and Maturation

But *Romeo and Juliet* has more to offer its viewers than a touching plot and engaging characters. A closer look will show that Shakespeare designed his play in such a way as to guide us skillfully toward a fuller understanding of its complexities, both in structure and in language. To observe this dramatic design, let us begin with the turning point we have already mentioned: the death of Mercutio.

The duel in which Mercutio and Tybalt are slain is central to the play not only in its placement at the beginning of Act III but also in its effect upon the populace of Verona. Mercutio is a pivotal figure for many reasons, including his own remarkable poetic imagination—so unlike that of others in the play—and the fact that he is a kinsman to the Prince, rather than to either the Montagues or the Capulets. It is no exaggeration to say that when he dies the world of *Romeo and Juliet* turns from comedy to tragedy. . . .

Juliet's Influence

In Act II, Scene iv, we see Mercutio engage Romeo in a battle of wits, rejoicing that his friend has become "sociable" once more. (The change in attitude, which Mercutio attributes to a return of common sense, has in fact resulted from Romeo's encounter with Juliet, and is yet another sign of her influence on his growth from self-absorption to self-knowledge.) As the puns and quips fly, Mercutio pretends to be overcome and finally calls upon a friend to part the combatants: "Come between us, good Benvolio! My wits faint" (66). The mood of the scene is comic, playful, and inconsequential—very like that of the first message scene between the Nurse and Juliet. But a few hours (and only three scenes) later, when the three friends encounter Tybalt, the same scenario results in tragedy. The weapons this time are swords rather than words, and it is Romeo who intervenes, while Mercutio is mortally wounded as a result of his intervention. Romeo's murmured explanation, "I thought all for the best" (III,i,102), tellingly reinforces the parallel between this duel and the previous one, for the name of Benvolio, the peacemaker in the duel of words, means literally "well-wisher"—one who "[thinks] all for the best."

We have mentioned a growth and change in Romeo, signified not only by his desire to heal the rift between the warring parties but also by a new vigor and originality in his language, profoundly different from the hackneyed phrases in which he expressed his passion for Rosaline. The most remarkable pattern of maturation in the play, however, is not Romeo's but Juliet's; indeed, it would not be excessive to say that she is the central figure in the play, despite the symmetrical balance of Montague with Capulet, or the even-handed justice of the title. And here again the playwright tips his hand—we must think, deliberately—by designing a series of steps by which the audience can clearly see a child become a woman. When we recall that the breakneck pace of *Romeo and Juliet* makes the entire drama occur within the course of four days, the transformation is even more astounding.

From Child to Woman

Juliet's growth to maturity is especially vivid for the audience because when first we see her she seems to have so far to go. In the opening scenes of the play she is wholly submissive, even passive, her sheltered life dominated by three authority figures: father, mother, and Nurse. Asked by her mother what she thinks of marriage, she replies "It is an honor that I dream not of (I,ii,66). When she is told that Paris seeks to marry her, her answer is similarly dutiful: "I'll look to like, if looking liking move (97)—but only, she hastens to add, if her mother gives consent. Given this initial glimpse of what is clearly a daughter rather than a mature woman, it is all the more startling for the audience to see what happens when first she sets eyes upon Romeo.

In the course of the Capulet ball, Juliet has spoken with Romeo and kissed him, but she does not yet know who he is. In order to find out, she devises a cleverly indirect ploy, first inquiring from the Nurse about the identities of two other young men in whom she actually has no interest. Only after she has learned their names, and thus diverted the Nurse's curiosity, does she ask about Romeo. Here for the first time we see Juliet act less than straightforwardly with one of her mentors, and in doing so begin to establish a separate adult identity. In a similar way, when her parents inform her of the marriage arranged with Paris, she replies with both overt defiance and covert cunning. "I will not marry yet," she tells her mother, "And when I do, I swear/It shall be Romeo, whom you know I hate,/Rather than Paris" (III,v,122-4).

Juliet's Isolation

From the time of this first meeting, but more particularly from the time of the tragic duel, Shakespeare shows us a Juliet whose self-knowledge is coupled with an increasing isolation, which separates her from friends and family, and leaves her, after Romeo's banishment, almost entirely on her own. As she develops from childhood to adulthood she undergoes a painful process of divestiture, stripping herself of former confidants one by one, as each appears to fail her. First she is forced to reject her parents, who insist blindly upon her marrying Paris; then, with even more pain, she must estrange herself from the Nurse, who though an essential ally in happier days, now cheerfully urges her to commit bigamy. In effect Juliet, too, is "banished" by the Prince's edict. In dramatic terms, her isolation is symbolized by such events as the two soliloquies she speaks from the balcony (II,ii; III,ii), her refusal—on the Friar's order—to let the Nurse sleep in her chamber on the eve of the wedding, and her poignant observation as she reaches for the sleeping potion: "My dismal scene I needs must act alone" (IV,iii,19). Although she is for a moment tempted to call to her mother and Nurse for comfort she realizes that the possibility of such comfort is lost. Finally, in the play's last scene, she will reject the Friar's inadequate though well-meant offer to "dispose" of her "among a sisterhood of holy nuns" (V,iii,156–7), and with it she rejects the Friar himself. This dismal scene, too, she must act alone.

But at the same time that she has lost her family and friends, she has gained a husband and lover—and in her scenes with Romeo, Juliet demonstrates a startling maturity of another kind by rejecting false modesty in favor of a frank declaration of love and an even franker declaration of sexual desire. The play invites us to contrast this behavior not only with her own previous naivete ("I'll look to like, if looking liking move") but also with the coy chastity of Romeo's first love, Rosaline, and with the coarse vulgarity of the Nurse. Thus, in the balcony scene Juliet is at first embarrassed to find that Romeo has overheard her private thoughts, but within half a dozen lines her "maiden blush" has given way to a direct and unashamed question: "Dost thou love me?" (II,ii,86; 90). Notice that it is she who asks the question, as it is she who has first spoken of love. Throughout the scene she remains the dominant figure, alternately advising, cautioning, and summoning Romeo, while he quite appropriately stands gazing at her from below. For a young woman of her age and her sheltered upbringing, this innocent forwardness is as remarkable as it is appealing. . . .

Society's Impediments

From the first, the audience is made aware that there is something seriously wrong in the play's world. The Chorus delivers a Prologue in the form of a sonnet, a fourteen-line poem usually devoted in Shakespeare's time to a private declaration of love. But here we have a sonnet gone public, and a sonnet that speaks not of love but of civil war: "Where civil blood makes civil hands unclean" (4). Moreover, the Prologue is followed by the appearance of two servants of the house of Capulet who seem to have no object in life except to quarrel with their rivals, the servants of Montague. . . . Their squabble inevitably expands to envelop their masters, as Old Capulet, still wearing his nightgown, rushes into the street calling for his sword. There could be no more visible sign of the disorder endemic in Verona than the fact that servants draw masters into battle rather than the other way around.

As always in Shakespeare's plays, civil war is a symbol of conflict, not only within nations or cities, but also within individuals. As Verona is torn apart by the "ancient grudge" (Prologue, 3) between the Montagues and the Capulets, so will Prince Escalus be torn between strict justice and generous mercy, Juliet torn between loyalty to her family and love for her husband, Romeo torn between a desire to halt the feud and a need to avenge the death of his friend Mercutio. . . .

In fact, it may be useful for us to look at the feud between the Montagues and the Capulets not only as the central political fact of the plot but also as an underlying pattern that determines the nature of theme, image, and language throughout the play. . . .

The presence of Old Capulet and Old Montague in the thick of the battle also reminds us of the tension that develops in this play between youth and age. Prince Escalus, parting the sides, speaks of "ancient citizens" who "wield old partisans, in hands as old," forsaking the gravity proper to their years (I,i,90; 92). At the ball we hear from Old Capulet himself that he is long past his dancing days, and the conflict of generations is heightened by the evident age of both the Friar and the Nurse. Romeo argues that the Friar cannot understand love since he is no longer young, and the Nurse complains volubly about her aching bones and shortness of breath. "Old folks," says Juliet, are "unwieldly, slow, heavy, and pale as lead" (II,v,16–17). Ironically the old men and women in the play often behave like children—impetuous, willful, and dogmatic—while some of the children possess a wisdom and maturity foreign to their parents. Yet the older generation wield the power in Verona, though the younger men—to their cost—bear the swords.

The two oppositions we have noticed are in some way analogous to one another; we might perhaps say that love is to death as youth is to age.

Growing Up
Outside Convention

Derek Traversi

Derek Traversi, who died in 2005 at the age of ninety-two, worked across Europe for the British Council (a cultural and educational organization) while establishing a position as a Shakespearean scholar. His most formidable accomplishment was the multivolume Approach to Shakespeare.

Derek Traversi begins the following essay by noting the similarity of Shakespeare's early sonnets to Romeo and Juliet *in style, imagery, and theme, in a drama regarding the nature of love in adversity. He proceeds with an analysis of the play, concentrating on the young lovers' clash with tradition and society in a violent, feuding world. In general, Traversi follows the growing maturity of Romeo and Juliet as they assert the primacy of their love against the conventional wisdom of their elders and friends. This is a setting in which young men, urged on by their elders, are always looking for a fight, and "experience" is a negative state pitted against "innocence." While Juliet grows from childhood, Romeo, transformed by love, grows beyond the conventional pattern of love, represented by Rosaline.*

The Prologue strikes a sinister note from the outset by telling us that we are about to witness 'the *fearful* passage of a *death-marked* love'; but it is necessary to add that the disaster to which this love will be brought is in great part a result of the hatred of the older generations, in which the young participate, if at all, as victims involved in a situation which is not of their choosing. Though the young lovers are indeed

Derek Traversi, "*Romeo and Juliet*," in *An Approach to Shakespeare: "I Henry VI" to "Twelfth Night,"* London: Hollis & Carter, 1968. This edition © Derek Traversi 1968. Reproduced by permission of Random House Group Limited, U.K. and Random House, Inc. for U.S.

'star-crossed', destined to die, their response to experience, and the contrast with those around them who only *believe* that they are reasonable and mature, gives the relationship to which they have pledged their generosity a proper measure of validity. Their love must indeed accept the reality of death, which its very origin and nature demand; but once this has been accepted, it remains true that a sense of incommensurate worth, of *true* value, survives to colour their tragedy.

The Prologue has no sooner been spoken when the circumstances which will lead fatally to the destruction of love are introduced in the shape of the irrational vanity of the Capulet-Montague feud. The serving-men who so touchily eye one another in the streets of Verona are at once lecherous and self-important, uneasily conscious of breaking what they know to be the law even as they insult their opposites. The masters, on this first showing, are little or no better than their men, combining touchiness and senility in a particularly distasteful way. Their wives know them better than themselves; when Capulet testily calls for his sword to join in the *melee*, his wife says ironically: 'A crutch, a crutch! why call you for a sword!' (I.i.82), and Lady Montague is equally at pains to hold back her husband from 'seeking a foe'. On the more active side, reason is habitually overruled by brute instinct, Benvolio's sensible attitude—'I do but keep the peace'—balanced by Tybalt's irrational spoiling for a fight: 'I hate hell, all Montagues, and thee!' (I.i.77). The fair comment on so much obstinate and 'canker'd hate' is left here, as it will be throughout the play, to Prince Escalus, who shows himself conscious, as an impartial ruler, of the ruin to which these senseless attitudes will lead, and who does what he can to hold them in check. We may conclude by the end of this opening that, if this is a fair picture of 'experience', there is likely to be something to be said in favour of the romantic idealism of youth. . . .

At this point, and after some talk of Capulet's forthcoming feast, we turn from Romeo to Juliet, who is urged by her mother to think of marriage and who replies, in her still un-awakened simplicity: 'It is an honour that I dream not of' (I.iii.66). Juliet, indeed, is surrounded here, as she will be almost to the end of the play, by the 'experienced', by those who are always ready to give their advice on the proper conduct of her life. Such is the Nurse, with her combination of easy sentiment and deep-rooted cynicism, her belief, at once normal and senile in its discursive presentation, that love is a prompting of the flesh which is destined to find its social fulfilment in a suitably contrived marriage; such too is her own mother, who looks back complacently on the destiny which at some remote moment in the past gave her to Capulet and which she is ready to elevate, for her daughter's benefit, into a universal pattern. . . .

It is typical of Romeo that his first reference to Juliet should speak of her in terms of 'enrichment', the enhancing effect proper to beauty; significant too that his first reaction to the sight of her should give him the force to break through all former artifice, to rise to what, though still romantic in inspiration, is in effect a new intensity:

O, she doth teach the torches to burn bright!

It seems she hangs upon the cheek of night

Like a rich jewel in an Ethiop's ear; (I.v.48)

a beauty capable, indeed, of transforming life, but which he can also, with what is already a sense of foreboding, hail immediately afterwards as 'Beauty too rich for use, for earth too dear'. Already, moreover, the world is ominously present at the birth of this new vision, and answers to the lover's rapt confession of his transformed state—'I ne'er saw true beauty till this night'—with Tybalt's harsh recognition—'This, by his voice, should be a Montague'—even as he calls for his sword. The sinister note has been struck once and for all, briefly but not at that account less powerfully, in spite of Capulet's determination that his feast shall not be interrupted, and in spite of the confrontation of Romeo's unruly enemy with the old man's stubborn 'will'. Yet again, as will occur so often in this play, age and youth, authority and passion meet, as Capulet's angry assertion of his right to command—'Am I the master here? or you?. . .

. . . Because this new love bears within itself an element of excess, a neglect of all realities except those which its own consummation involves, it will end in death; but because it is also a true motion (and true not least in relation to the aged experience that sets itself up so consistently to thwart it, to deny its truth), because its intensity answers, when all has been said, to love's *value*, it will be felt to achieve, even in its inevitable frustration, a certain measure of triumph over circumstance.

The element of contradiction makes its presence felt throughout this famous scene. Juliet, here as nearly always a good deal more realistic than Romeo, knows from the first that their love is surrounded by a sinister reality which its material circumstances confirm:

The orchard walls are high and hard to climb,

And the place death, considering who thou art; (II.ii.63)

to which his passionate reply is at once, when viewed in terms of worldly common-sense, a further expression of excess, and, in relation to the new vision which has taken possession of him, a sign of the nature of true love:

With love's light wings did I o'erperch these walls,

For stony limits cannot hold love out:

And what love can do, that dares love attempt. (II.ii.66)

The Romeo who speaks after this fashion, and who goes on to say:

wert thou as far

As that vast shore wash'd with the farthest sea,

I would adventure for such merchandise. (II.ii.82)

is clearly a new person in relation to the conventional lover whom Mercutio and his friends could justly ridicule in the opening scenes. His eyes have been opened to the reality of love as an 'adventure', involving the total commitment of self, the willingness to risk all to obtain the rich 'merchandise', the prize of great value which love—if in fact it is a central reality in human experience—implies. This gesture of the gift of self, however, is at once necessary and dangerous, balanced over a void. This is recognized again, and in a new way, by Juliet when she answers Romeo's entranced declarations with a direct simplicity of her own and calls for an answering directness and simplicity from her lover:

O gentle Romeo,

If thou dost love, pronounce it faithfully. (II.ii.93)

Romeo's far-flung declarations of the value and intensity of love call, as their natural counterpart, for plainer, more naturally human decisions, and it is these which Juliet is here emphasizing. By so doing, she does not, of course, call in question the truth and validity of the emotions which have transported Romeo to what is in effect a new life; but she is saying that these transports call for translation into a more intimate key, demand incorporation into a more common, but not on that account a less precious or valid reality. . . .

It is significant that . . . when the course of events can clearly be seen passing beyond the lovers' possible control, that Juliet shows more clearly than ever before how far she has developed beyond the unawakened adolescent of the opening scenes. If she now calls upon 'love-performing night', it is

Still scene from the 1968 film version of Romeo and Juliet *with Olivia Hussey as Juliet with Natasha Parry as her mother.* The Kobal Collection/The Picture Desk, Inc.

in no mere prolongation of the earlier romantic exchanges— and, indeed, in this sense it has always been Romeo, rather than herself, who has felt so intensely the attractions of the extinction of light—but in search of the full physical consummation of her love. Her words are in this sense precise and firm:

O, I have bought the mansion of a love,

But not possess'd it, and, though I am sold,

Not yet enjoy'd; so tedious is this day

As is the night before some festival

To an impatient child that hath new robes

And may not wear them. (III.ii.26)...

'Experience' . . . in the grosser and more insensitive form represented by old Capulet, is busy about its own short-sighted plans. 'Well, we were born to die' is his characteristic comment on Tybalt's death, and it is decided that Juliet, in order to shake her from her supposed grief for the dead man, shall be bundled as quickly as possible into marriage with Paris. Once again, facile good intentions serve only to hasten disaster. It is against this ominous background that Romeo and Juliet achieve (III.v) the brief consummation of their mutual love. It is a consummation, as we now have reason to expect, which is at once intense, contradictory, and finally poised over fear: fear, above all, for the future, whilst life is being plucked, in intense and breathless haste, from the insubstantial present. The nightingale sings, for Juliet, in 'the *fearful* hollow' of her lover's ear, and Romeo, exultant as he is in the moment of achievement—

Night's candles are burnt out, and *jocund* day

Stands tip-toe on the misty mountain tops— (III.v.9)

can only precariously maintain his happiness. 'I must be gone and live, or stay and die'. Life is, for him, with Juliet, and absence from her means death; so that, when Juliet, as ever more realistic at heart, clings desperately to what she knows to be an illusion—'thou needst not to be gone'—he is ready to deny truth in the name of his love: 'I'll say yon grey is not the morning's eye'. Once again, however, the end of love is foreseen to lie in death: 'Come, death, and welcome! Juliet wills it so'. Even, however, as Romeo accepts the illusion upon which his life now rests, it is Juliet who returns to daily reality—'It is the lark that sings so out of tune'—and who foresees that they must separate. Truth, in other words, stands most delicately balanced against illusion; to decide which is which, and to what end they are interwoven, could be described as precisely the *crux* of this tragedy. As Juliet admits that 'more light and light it grows', it is left to Romeo to make his comment of tragic foreboding: 'More light and light: more dark and dark our woes'.

At this point reality intervenes in yet another form, as the Nurse interrupts the lovers to bring news, with day-break, of the approach of Lady Capulet. There is once again an ominous note in Juliet's last question, 'thinkst thou we shall ever meet again?'; and though Romeo's reply seems to suggest confidence—

I doubt it not; and all these woes shall serve

For sweet discourses in our time to come— (III.v.52)

the sinister death note reaffirms itself in the last words which, in the event, Juliet will speak to her lover alive:

O God! I have an ill-divining soul.

Methinks I see thee, now thou art below,

As one dead in the bottom of a tomb. (III. v. 54)

At the last she is left to rely upon fortune—that deity 'fickle' in the eyes of the world, tending at all times to impose separation—to send Romeo back to her arms.

The world beyond the lovers proceeds, meanwhile, on its own paths of misunderstanding. Lady Capulet believes that her daughter weeps for Tybalt and often, in typically 'experienced' terms, her moralizing consolation:

some grief shows much of love,

But much of grief shows still some want of wit.

As always, 'experience' seeks the solution to all problems in 'moderation': seeks it precisely where love, of its very nature, is unable to find it. It is noteworthy, however, as a sign of the way in which the complexities of maturity are imposing themselves, that when Romeo is mentioned, Juliet shows herself old enough to dissemble to her mother. 'Indeed', she says,

I never shall be satisfied

With Romeo, till I behold him—dead; (III.v.95)

what she does not know, and what constitutes, of course, the irony of this situation, is that this 'satisfaction' is very shortly to be granted her. Her mother, meanwhile, has come to bring her news of the 'wedding' which has been arranged by the elderly and the 'experienced' for what they have decided is her own good; and her more formidable father now enters to confirm his 'decree'. At this point, we are clearly shown the fundamental insensibility of those who claim to be versed in the ways of the world: shown it nowhere more obviously than in Capulet's unreasoning rage at Juliet's timid attempts to cross him—'My fingers itch!'—and scarcely less evidently in her own mother's callous remark: 'I would the fool were married to her grave'. And so, indeed, she shall be, sooner than Lady Capulet knows; but meanwhile the Nurse is allowed to utter her protest in the name of a certain human feeling—'You are to blame, my lord, to rate her so'—only to evoke the father's egoistic stressing of what he believes to be his own unrewarded care and toil:

Day, night, hour, tide, time, work, play,

Alone, in company, still my care hath been

To have her match'd. (III.v.178)

It is, in fact, his own self-esteem which feels itself affronted by his daughter's obstinacy, and which prompts him to turn her away unless she is docile to his will. Juliet, indeed, faced by a situation slipping beyond all possible control, feels herself caught in a trap:

Alack, alack, that heaven should practise stratagems

Upon so soft a subject as myself; (III.v.211)

but when she seeks advice from the Nurse, who has so recently shown her some measure of understanding, it is only to be told that Romeo is a 'dishclout' in comparison with Paris; there is point indeed in her own final disenchanted comment: 'Well, thou hast comforted me marvellous much'.

Thus abandoned by those from whom she might have expected help, Juliet decides to turn to the Friar, only—by yet another ironic mischance—to find Paris, her discreet and honourable suitor, in advance of her at his cell. Even as she asks for counsel, she already sees her ultimate 'solution' in the death which is pressing itself upon her intimate reflections. Rather than be forced to marry Paris, she says,

> shut me nightly in a charnel-house,
>
> O'ercovered quite with dead men's rattling bones,
>
> With reeking shanks and yellow chapless skulls;
>
> Or bid me go into a new-made grave,
>
> And hide me with a dead man in his shroud;
>
> Things that to hear them told, have made me tremble.
> (IV.i.81)

Her thoughts are full of the charnel-house, the obsessive presence which will from now on live in her mind side by side with love. Precisely these things, which she now regards with horror, she is fated to do; but we should recognize too that these forebodings, excessive as they are, are spoken in the name of loving faith:

> I will do it without fear or doubt,
>
> To live an unstain'd wife to my sweet love. (IV.i.87)

Strong in the love which this determination reflects, Juliet is able at this crisis to dissemble beyond her years. Her deception of her father, in the very act of professing filial obedience (IV.ii), is no doubt a sin, but a sin conceived in the name of natural love and in the face of an egoistic and unimaginative opposition; once more, we find ourselves faced with the play's central tragic contradiction. To affirm the rights of love, Juliet finds herself driven to dissemble; her situation is one which can, of its nature, have no happy solution, but we cannot—unless we are ready to share the egoism and incomprehension of her parents—simply leave her condemned of deception. . . .

Coming of Age in Verona

Coppélia Kahn

Coppélia Kahn, professor of English and gender studies at Brown University, is the author of Changing Subjects: The Making of Feminist Literary Criticism *(1993) and the president of the Shakespeare Association of America (2008–09).*

Coppélia Kahn, in giving a feminist interpretation of Romeo and Juliet *in the following essay, places the blame for the catastrophic development not on the acts or the normal and natural impulses of the young lovers, but rather on the feud, which is their social milieu in Verona, and especially on the parents. Both Capulets and Montagues neglect their offspring while assuming that each will follow the customs of the times, dictated by intolerance, social divisions, and the patriarchal society that, Kahn asserts, is "tragically self-destructive." Kahn's analysis covers the development and maturation of Romeo and Juliet within this restricted and fateful environment, which includes the spirited young people who surround Romeo and the domestic isolation of Juliet. Romeo follows the pattern of "courtly love" in his infatuation for Rosaline, but Juliet's first experience is with Romeo.*

Romeo and Juliet is about a pair of adolescents trying to grow up. Growing up requires that they separate themselves from their parents by forming with a member of the opposite sex an intimate bond which supersedes filial bonds. This, broadly, is an essential task of adolescence, in Renaissance England and Italy as in America today, and the play is particularly concerned with the social milieu in which these adolescent lovers grow up—a patriarchal milieu as English as

Coppélia Kahn, "Coming of Age in Verona," in *The Woman's Part: Feminist Criticism of Shakespeare*, ed. Carolyn Ruth Swift Lenz, Gayle Greene, and Carol Thomas Neely, Champaign: University of Illinois Press, 1980, pp. 171–193. Copyright © 1980 by the Board of Trustees of the University of Illinois. Reproduced by permission of the author.

it is Italian. I shall argue that the feud in a realistic social sense is the primary tragic force in the play—not the feud as agent of fate, but the feud as an extreme and peculiar expression of patriarchal society, which Shakespeare shows to be tragically self-destructive. The feud is the deadly *rite de passage* that promotes masculinity at the price of life. Undeniably, the feud is bound up with a pervasive *sense* of fatedness, but that sense finds its objective correlative in the dynamics of the feud and of the society in which it is embedded. . . .

The Feud

That inheritance makes Romeo and Juliet tragic figures because it denies their natural needs and desires as youth. Of course, they also display the faults of youth: its self-absorption and reckless extremism, its headlong surrender to eros. But it is the feud which fosters the rash, choleric impulsiveness typical of youth by offering a permanent invitation to and outlet for violence. The feud is first referred to in the play as "their parents strife and their parents' rage" and it is clear that the parents, not their children, are responsible for its continuance. Instead of providing social channels and moral guidance by which the energies of youth can be rendered beneficial to themselves and society, the Montagues and the Capulets make weak gestures toward civil peace while participating emotionally in the feud as much as their children do. While they fail to exercise authority over the younger generation in the streets, they wield it selfishly and stubbornly in the home. So many of the faults of character which critics have found in Romeo and Juliet are shared by their parents that the play cannot be viewed as a tragedy of character in the Aristotelian sense, in which the tragedy results because the hero and heroine fail to "love moderately." Rather, the feud's ambiance of hot temper permeates age as well as youth; viewed from the standpoint of Prince Escalus, who embodies the law, it is Montague and Capulet who are childishly refractory.

In the course of the action, Romeo and Juliet create and try to preserve new identities as adults apart from the feud, but it blocks their every attempt. Metaphorically, it devours them in the "detestable maw" of the Capulets' monument, a symbol of the patriarchy's destructive power over its children. Thus both the structure and the texture of the play suggest a critique of the patriarchal attitudes expressed through the feud, which makes "tragic scapegoats" of Romeo and Juliet.

Specifically, for the sons and daughters of Verona the feud constitutes socialization into patriarchal roles in two ways. First, it reinforces their identities as sons and daughters by allying them with their paternal household against another paternal household, thus polarizing all their social relations, particularly their marital choices, in terms of filial allegiance. . . .

Conception of Manhood

The conflict between [Mercutio's] conception of manhood and the one which Romeo learns is deftly and tellingly suggested in Romeo's line, "He jests at scars that never felt a wound" (II.i.I). Juliet is a Capulet, and Romeo risks death to love her; the trite metaphor of the wound of love has real significance for him. Mercutio considers love mere folly unworthy of a real man and respects only the wounds suffered in combat. Ironically, Mercutio will die of a real wound occasioned partly by Romeo's love, while Romeo, no less a man, will die not of a wound but of the poison he voluntarily takes for love.

Mercutio mocks not merely the futile, enfeebling kind of love Romeo feels for Rosaline, but all love. Moreover, his volley of sexual innuendo serves as the equivalent of both fighting and love. In its playful way, his speech is as aggressive as fighting, and while speech establishes his claim to virility, at the same time it marks his distance from women. As Romeo says, Mercutio is "A gentleman . . . that loves to hear himself talk and will speak more in a minute than he will stand to in a month" [II.iv.153–55]. Mercutio would rather fight than talk, but he would rather talk than love. . . .

In patriarchal Verona, men bear names and stand to fight for them; women, "the weaker vessels," bear children and "fall backward" to conceive them, as the Nurse's husband once told the young Juliet. It is appropriate that Juliet's growing up is hastened and intensified by having to resist the marriage arranged for her by her father, while Romeo's is precipitated by having to fight for the honor of his father's house. Unlike its sons, Verona's daughters have, in effect, no adolescence, no sanctioned period of experiment with adult identities or activities. . . .

Patriarchal Terms

Shakespeare, by introducing the arranged marriage at the beginning and by making Capulet change his mind about it, shows us how capricious patriarchal rule can be, and how the feud changes fatherly mildness to what Hartley Coleridge called "paternal despotism." After Tybalt's death, the marriage which before required her consent is now his "decree," and his anger at her opposition mounts steadily from an astonished testiness to brutal threats:

> And you be mine, I'll give you to
> my friend;
> And you be not, hang, beg, starve,
> die in the streets,
> For, by my soul, I'll ne'er acknowl-
> edge thee,
> Nor what is mine shall never do
> thee good. (III.v.193–96)

Surrogate Parents

Romeo finds a surrogate father outside the [patriarchal] system, in Friar Lawrence, and in fact never appears onstage with his parents. Juliet, on the other hand, always appears within her parents' household until the last scene in the tomb. Lodged in the bosom of the family, she has two mothers, the Nurse as well as her real one. For Juliet, the Nurse is the opposite of what the Friar is for Romeo; she is a surrogate mother within the patriarchal family, but one who is, finally, of little help in assisting Juliet in her passage from child to woman. She embodies the female self molded devotedly to the female's family role. The only history she knows is that of birth, suckling, weaning, and marriage; for her, earthquakes are less cataclysmic than these turning points of growth. She and Juliet enter the play simultaneously in a scene in which she has almost all the lines and Juliet less than ten, a disproportion which might be considered representative of the force of tradition weighing on the heroine. . . .

Love and Death

The lovers want to live in union; the death-dealing feud opposes their desire. The tragic conclusion, however, effects a complete turnabout in this clear-cut opposition between love and death, for in the lovers' suicides love and death merge. Romeo and Juliet die as an act of love, in a spiritualized acting out of the ancient pun [in which "to die" also means to have sexual consummation]. Furthermore, the final scene plays off against each, consumed and destroyed by the feud, and that they rise above it, united in death. The ambivalence of this conclusion is worth exploring to see how it reflects the play's concern with coming of age in the patriarchal family. . . .

A Fatal Coming of Age

Shakespeare fills Romeo's last speech with the imagery of life's richness: the gloomy vault is "a feasting presence full of light," and Juliet's lips and cheeks are crimson with vitality. His last lines, "O true apothecary! / Thy drugs are quick. Thus with a kiss I die" (v.iii.120), bring together the idea of death as sexual consummation and as rebirth. Similarly, Juliet kisses the poison on his lips and calls it "a restorative." They have come of age by a means different from the rites of passage—phallic violence and adolescent motherhood—typical for youth in Verona. Romeo's death in the tomb of the Capulets rather than in that of his own fathers reverses the traditional passage of the female over to the male house in marriage and betokens his refusal to follow the code of his fathers. And it is Juliet, not Romeo, who boldly uses his dagger against herself.

Becoming a Man

Robert Appelbaum

Robert Appelbaum is a lecturer in Renaissance studies at Lancaster University in England. He is the author of Envisioning an English Empire *(2004).*

In the following article, Robert Appelbaum sees Romeo and Juliet *as being driven by the necessity of growing up within a hard and violent "masculine performance" that dominates the play and determines the tragedy. For Romeo, this crude view of manhood is both necessary and unreachable. The embodiments of this concept are Prince Escalus and the fathers of the young lovers. The patriarchy declares that this kind of manliness makes possible "civil love and civil peace," but it is in fact aggressive, chaotic, and juvenile. The basic idea of what it means to be a man is inherent from the opening, in which the quarreling servants reveal their confrontational machismo. Yet this way of life is completely incompatible with Romeo and Juliet's love. Romeo must grow up in this fierce code of masculinity. He and Juliet do become adults, but the social code is the opposite of love and leads to their tragic ends.*

Th[e] dilemma of masculinity is rehearsed in the often-cited masculinist patter that opens *Romeo and Juliet* and leads to a renewal of violence in the world of the play. "To move is to stir, and to be valiant is to stand," the Capulet servant Gregory argues, preparing to incite a brawl. But what is a man, then, really to do? To stir or to stand? The assertive masculinity that Gregory is trying to grasp immediately slips out of his hands and out of his words, since to stand, as his companion, Sampson, rejoins, is to "take the wall," and yet "the

Robert Appelbaum, "'Standing to the Wall,' The Pressures of Masculinity in *Romeo and Juliet*," *Shakespeare Quarterly* (Baltimore, MD), vol. 48, 1997, pp. 251–272.

weakest goes to the wall"; the wall is a place for women (1.1.9–14). To be a man is to move, to stir, to push, to thrust ("I will push Montague's men from the wall, and thrust his maids to the wall" [l.l.16–17]); but it is also to stand, to show oneself standing, "to show [oneself] a tyrant," and attempt to exact tribute to one's masculinity, to secure ratification that one is standing: "My naked weapon is out"; "I will frown as I pass by, and let them take it as they list" (l.l.21,34,41). On the one hand, the man wants to take up the position that is already waiting for him, the position of his own lack; he wants to stir and occupy it, displacing his rivals, abusing their women. On the other hand, the man wants to wear the mask of having the position occupied; he wants to show himself not stirring toward it but already standing there in possession of his masculinity. Valiantly standing, he is confirmed, at last, in his manhood. Or is he?

It is clear from its context that the rivalry between the Capulets and the Montagues is also, for the men, the impetus for an inward rivalry, an inward pressure to masculine self-assertion that cannot be appeased or concluded.

Regime of Masculinity

In the world of *Romeo and Juliet* the regime of masculinity is constituted as a system from which there is no escape, but in keeping with which there is no experience of masculine satisfaction either, although the drama played out by Romeo may seduce us into thinking that there is both one and the other.

One might continue this line of inquiry by looking into the nature of the alternatives themselves. What would it mean for a male *not* to be a man in the world of *Romeo and Juliet*, to be a male subject without being a captive of the masculinist regime?

Heterosexual Love

Certainly Romeo and Juliet believe that they can bypass the boundaries of this system—leaping over walls; standing "proof" against the "enmity" of their families; Juliet vowing to lay at Romeo's feet a fortune that is not in her power to bequeath or, when threatened by her official engagement to Count Paris, to "leap . . . / From off the battlements of any tower" (4.1.77–78). But their belief in escape is, again, an expression of the system that determines them. The system itself is complex, and those very endpoints of value toward one might incline in order to bypass the limits of masculinist aggression—civil peace and heterosexual love—are among the system's constitutive normative elements. The *mise-en-abyme* ["putting into infinity"; i.e., repeating, reflecting themes] of masculinist aggression that individuals such as Sampson, Gregory, and Tybalt are determined to embrace is part of the same system that permits Prince Escalus, speaking from a position of unquestioned authority, to condemn them for their "pernicious rage" (1.1.84). And it is part of the same system that leads Romeo—with the oxymoronic acceleration that characterizes his affair with Juliet—to "stand on sudden haste" (2.2.94) and pursue his passion to his death. . . . If endless cycles of violence are expressions of the regime of masculinity, so is the promulgation of the law, a law of peace, which itself has the right to resort to violence ("*On pain of torture*, from those bloody hands / Throw your mistempered weapons to the ground" [1.1.86–87, emphasis added]). So, too, is the promulgation of the idea of an alternative, the idea of standing apart from the masculinist regime in practices of heterosexual love. . . .

The young men in *Romeo and Juliet* are not, as men, *in control of themselves*; they are not in control of the project of masculine autonomy to which they understand themselves to be pledged. Autonomy, to be sure, along with the circumstances under which it can be imagined or asserted, is a problem with which Shakespearean characters are often confronted. But the idea of an explicitly masculine autonomy is especially troublesome for Shakespearean characters. Masculinity is not a single thing they can get a hold of, although they are constantly under pressure to do so. Masculinity is rather a regime.... They have to go forward, they have to stir ... they also have to remain in that third position, from which they embark in pursuit of their objectives, the self. "I have lost myself," Romeo complains in his opening scene; "I am not here" (1.1.197).... The men want to achieve the endpoints of their masculinist system, but that system proves to be one of male inadequacy and incompletion, a system blowing masculine selves from their selves....

It is not for nothing that, in chiding Romeo, Friar Laurence argues against both Romeo's womanly grief and his beastly rage: "thy wild acts," the friar adds, "denote / The unreasonable fury of a beast" (3.3.110–11). The manliness the friar wants Romeo to exemplify is a condition of self-directedness and self-control: it is not only a way of not being a woman; it is also a way of not being a lower animal....

Sacrificed to State Masculinity

In *Romeo and Juliet*, in spite of all the disorderly conduct that constitutes the main action of the play, the context of masculinist patriarchy is particularly well marked. The symbolic role of the dead father is supplied by the living Prince Escalus, who in practice is an absolute monarch. "If ever you disturb our streets again," he says to the street fighters, "Your lives shall pay the forfeit of the peace" (1.1.96–97). Strong words, and not the words that a relatively restricted monarch such as the sovereign prince of England would be entitled to pronounce. Escalus is represented as being at once the principle of law and order in his society and its principal enforcer, holding in his person judicial, legislative, and executive powers all at once.... If the town is subject to the contagion of what the Prologue calls an "ancient grudge" (1.3), a contagion clearly calling for purgative elimination, it is nonetheless invulnerable to decay from without; and it has never experienced an outbreak of disorder such as to threaten legal and social stability. Indeed, it is precisely because the symbolic order of the law is historically invulnerable that the "ancient grudge" can be resolved by a purgative cleansing—the sacrifice of Romeo and Juliet on the altar of civic life—rather than by warfare. The prince may have his hands full maintaining order between the Capulets and the Montagues, but he doesn't need to worry about maintaining legality between his subjects and himself. The primary *symbolic* order of Verona is safe because the "dead Father" of Verona is also alive and, as Henry V was (and as James I would soon claim to be), capable of enforcing the law by the exercise of violence.

Against the sovereign masculinity of Prince Escalus, however, the play juxtaposes the compromised masculinity and sovereignty of its "Rebellious subjects, enemies to peace," as Escalus calls them (1.1.31)—the other men of the play, clinging to their varied, unresolved, inadequate masculinities. Among them are the other father figures of the play: Capulet, Montague, and Friar Laurence, none of whom can succeed in establishing himself as a "speaking law." Capulet is temperamental and capricious, at times indulgent, at times an impatient martinet, and wholly ineffectual. Sometimes we find him asserting his patriarchal prerogatives benevolently, or at least pretending to do so, as when he insists on allowing Juliet some freedom in her choice of spouse (1.2.17—19) or on allowing Romeo to be a guest at his party (1.5.65–74). . . .

Father and Sons

Yet, when his power is challenged, Capulet is unable to exercise it without giving in to what amounts to ineffectual hysteria; he cannot manipulate the system of deference and courtesy through which he has otherwise pledged himself to manage his social and familial affairs. "Hang thee, young baggage! disobedient wretch!" (3.5.160), he complains to Juliet when she tries to assert the autonomy he had earlier granted her and has now inexplicably determined to withhold. "Speak not, reply not, do not answer me! / My fingers itch" (1.1.163–64). Capulet is an exemplar of paternalism on trial; but as the action proceeds, his paternalism continually fails, his authority undermined by turns of events he cannot control, his composure shattered at the shattering of his expectations. There is little if any conquering virtue in him, although Capulet certainly wants to act as if there were, and as if his experience of social life were equal to his symbolic, legal position in it.

Montague is even less firm in his patriarchal standing. Diminished in his virility in part through old age, . . . he is shown to be incapable of stirring—either as the young men do, in search of his foe, or as a paternal figure might aspire to do, in search of exacting tribute to his dignity. "Hold me not, let me go," he complains to his wife as he first appears onstage. "Thou shalt not stir one foot to seek a foe," his wife decrees (1.1.79–80). This diminished figure is shown, moreover, to have little influence on his son, Romeo, who keeps himself, as Montague indulgently complains, "so secret and so close" (1.1.49). Romeo never once considers his father's wishes when engaging in his affair with Juliet. He never pauses before the law of his father.

As for Friar Laurence, to whom Romeo regularly turns instead: although the friar endeavors to promote a kind of order in the world of Verona, similar in virtue to the prince's, his methods are indirect, and both his position and his character, his inner virtue, are obviously suspect. He is a priest and an herbalist and a self-appointed supplement to Prince Escalus in his aim to bolster the social order as well as to minister to it. But the friar is in many respects the play's most salient example of a man who *gets it wrong*, who *fails* to achieve his objectives, although he ultimately finds that his one objective of reuniting the Capulets and the Montagues has been achieved *for* him, partly as a consequence of his own mistakes. . . .

The masculine order of Verona is thus represented as dispersed among a number of imperfect masculinities, tied together in a fundamentally stable structure, whose absolute legality is embodied in the person of the prince. At the top of this structure the prince guarantees the symbolic order of the law. Beneath him, we are given to understand, a number of "citizens" are available to rise to the occasion of guaranteeing the law as well. The citizens appear on the scene whenever violence breaks out and, along with the prince, restore the peace.... The fathers are ineffectual; the sons (and the sonlike servants) are self-destructive. The fathers cannot enforce their own laws; the sons can neither enforce those laws on behalf of their fathers nor discover adequate forms of self-assertion....

The men whom we come to know as men are under pressure, in effect, to *perform*. But the fathers cannot perform as fathers; the sons cannot perform as sons either for the sake of their fathers or for themselves.... The fathers cannot enforce the law so long as they themselves are living in a self-imposed condition of "mutiny" or "rebellion."...

As a male subject in a Shakespearean tragic universe, Romeo can only oscillate, now thrusting himself forward, now standing aloof, awaiting a ratification he cannot receive. Without that ratification he is headed toward death. It is in that death that he fulfills the highest ideals of the social order and its law-of-the-father, civil love and civil peace.... Living as a man in Shakespeare's world, in the flow of history, even within a town where history seems to have temporarily come to an end, Romeo discovers that the regime of masculine performance laid down for him has always been strangely separating from him, even though he cannot do without it.

Juliet's Right of Veto

Cedric Watts

Cedric Watts is a professor at the University of Sussex. His specialties are the works of Joseph Conrad and Graham Greene.

Cedric Watts examines in the following essay the questions of arranged marriage, as it is relevant to Romeo and Juliet. *He notes that the play favors the "right of veto," by which very young girls, like Juliet, can at least refuse the men chosen for them by their fathers. In supporting the right of veto, Shakespeare also rebukes the entire patriarchal system and the old conservative-royalist argument (advocated in church doctrine) that as God is ruler of the universe, so, in the secular sphere, the king is absolute ruler over his kingdom, and family patriarchs are absolute rulers over their children, even with regard to marriage. Old Capulet, representative of a repressive system, first questions whether Juliet is old enough for marriage, then arranges the marriage (giving her the right of veto), but finally rushes up the marriage and takes away her right of veto. The play, Watts says, is far more politically radical than is generally perceived.*

When she marries Romeo, Juliet is thirteen (within a fortnight of her fourteenth birthday): which, to modern audiences, may seem a bizarrely early age. Her eligibility for marriage receives quite detailed discussion in the play. Initially, Capulet seems reluctant to concede that she is ready for Paris:

> Let two more summers wither in
> their pride
> Ere we may think her ripe to be a
> bride.

Cedric Watts, "Sexual Politics," in *Twayne's New Critical Introductions to Shakespeare: "Romeo and Juliet,"* Boston: Twayne Publishers, 1991, pp. 89–116.

Paris counters with the observation: 'Younger than she are happy mothers made'; to which Capulet retorts: 'And too soon marr'd are those so early made'. Nevertheless, he grants Paris his provisional consent, and only two days later will be imperiously insistent on Juliet's speedy acquiescence. Lady Capulet cites her own marital career as evidence that Juliet is ripe and ready:

> Well, think of marriage now. Younger than you
>
> Here in Verona, ladies of esteem,
>
> Are made already mothers. By my count
>
> I was your mother much upon these years
>
> That you are now a maid.

The Marriageable Age

In Elizabethan England, the legal ages of consent were twelve for a female and fourteen for a male; but, among noble and wealthy families, marriages were often contracted for younger children. Carroll Camden, in *The Elizabethan Woman*, remarks:

> The age of fourteen seems to have been a popular one for the marriage of girls. . . . Overbury's character of a true woman relates: 'Shee is *Marriageable* and Foureteene at once; and after shee doth not liue, but tarry.'

Similarly, Camden points out, [Ben] Jonson's *The Magnetick Lady* suggests that fourteen is a ripe age for marriage. But this was a matter of debate: Alexander Nicholas claimed that fourteen was too early: dangerous births might ensue; and J.L. Vives argued that women should be at least eighteen before bearing children. Lawrence Stone, in *The Family, Sex and Marriage*, demonstrates that the earlier marriages tended to take place in the higher social strata, where considerations of property and dynastic power often influenced the parents, whereas the later marriages were increasingly common lower in the social scale, where there was little (if any) property at stake. He says that among the wealthy classes in the late sixteenth century, the average age at marriage for daughters was twenty, for sons twenty-two; while among the middle class and lower classes the equivalent ages were around twenty-four and twenty-six respectively. Six per cent of the English peerage married at fifteen or earlier. (In royal history, over the centuries, child brides had not been unusual: in 1396 Richard II had married the six-year-old Isabella of France; while Henry Bolingbroke, who was to depose Richard and become King Henry IV, had taken a bride who was no older than eleven, and who produced a baby within a year). It seems, then, that although a marriage at thirteen was certainly early, and a matter of debate among authorities, it would have been accepted as not unreasonable for a female child of the prosperous burgher class. In Shakespeare's *Pericles*, Marina marries at the age of fourteen; in *The Winter's Tale*, Perdita is about sixteen; and in *The Tempest*, Miranda is fifteen.

The Right of Veto

Lawrence Stone argues that, largely as a consequence of the rise of Protestantism with its polemical emphasis on the value of matrimony (in opposition to Catholicism, with its higher valuation of celibacy), there was an increasing, if still limited, recognition of the claims of the young person to an agreeable partner:

> At first, in the early sixteenth century, children were bought and sold like cattle for breeding, and no-one thought that the parties concerned had any right to complain. But Protestant moral theology, with its stress on 'holy matrimony'[,] slowly forced a modification of this extreme position, which was only maintained in its pure state through the seven-

teenth century in the highest ranks of the aristocracy where the stakes of property and power were largest. To retain 'holy matrimony', which the theologians thought desirable in itself, as well as being a way to reduce adultery, it was necessary that the couple should be able to develop some affection for each other. It was therefore thought necessary to concede to the children the right of veto, the right to reject a spouse chosen by the parents[,] on the grounds that the antipathy aroused by a single interview was too great to permit the possibility of the future development of affection. This right of veto could only be used with caution and probably only once, or at most twice, while for women there was always the risk that its exercise might condemn them to spinsterhood, if their parents failed to provide another suitor.

This account of the 'right of veto' tallies quite closely with what Shakespeare shows in *Romeo and Juliet*. Initially, Capulet tells Paris that he concedes to Juliet that privilege:

> But woo her, gentle Paris, get her
> heart,
>
> My will to her consent is but a
> part,
>
> And she agreed, within her scope
> of choice
>
> Lies my consent and fair according
> voice.

Of course, when Juliet exercises that right of veto, Capulet is infuriated and threatens to cast her out and disinherit her. . . .

Choice in Marriage

Official homilies for repetition in church, like the homily 'Against Disobedience and Wilful Rebellion', emphasised that

Still scene from the 1996 film version of Romeo and Juliet *with Leonardo Di Caprio as Romeo and Claire Danes as Juliet.* The Kobal Collection/The Picture Desk, Inc.

as God rules the universe, so the monarch rules the state and the father should rule the family. Henry Smith, an influential Protestant, asked:

> If children may not make other contracts without [parents'] good will, shall they contract marriage, which have nothing to maintain it after, unless they return to beg of them whom they scorned before?

But these very qualifications help us to see that *Romeo and Juliet* is a far more radically—and radical—political work than it first appears to be. The politics of the play are no mere matter of a feud between rival clans. In the ages-long religious, cultural and political dispute between those different valuations of marriage which may be approximately, though with many exceptions, correlated with Catholic and Protestant outlooks, Shakespeare's sympathies lay rather with the higher valuation often attributed by the Protestant; and in the vast political dispute between the principle of the arranged marriage and the principle that young people should freely choose their partners on the basis of mutual love, he sides powerfully with the emergent modern preference for free choice and mutuality. . . .

A cynic might wish to add the postscript that since Romeo and Juliet are dead within a few days of their clandestine marriage, this play actually offers a rebuke to rebellious lovers. That is not, however, how their death is interpreted at the close of the drama. It is seen as a reproach to the intolerance of the rival patriarchs, and even to the Prince who had failed to curb that patriarchal power. Coppélia Kahn has argued that *Romeo and Juliet* 'cannot be viewed as a tragedy of character in the Aristotelian sense, in which the tragedy results because the hero and heroine fail to "love moderately"', for the primary tragic force is 'the feud as an extreme and peculiar expression of patriarchal society, which Shakespeare shows to be tragically self-destructive':

> Metaphorically, it devours them in the 'detestable maw' of the Capulets' monument, a symbol of the patriarchy's destructive power over its children.

Yet patriarchy stands rebuked, and the play gives strong moral endorsement to Romeo and Juliet: their golden statues will endure side by side as symbols of a love which disregards the pride and prejudice of kin and clan.

Recent historical and sociological studies suggest that *Romeo and Juliet* may afford a more accurate insight into the cultural trends of Shakespeare's period than Lawrence Stone's work indicated; and they also vindicate the cultural force of a play which, at a time when the authority of parents (aided by those clerics who frowned on fleshly passions) was increasingly challenged by the inclinations of young lovers, sided strongly and influentially with the latter.

A Daughter's Rebellion

Sharon Hamilton

Sharon Hamilton is chair of the English department at Buckingham Brown and Nichols School in Cambridge, Massachussetts.

Sharon Hamilton's following essay studies thirteen-year-old Juliet's rebellion against her materialistic father, who, within the tradition of the times, sees himself as an absolute lord over his family. Capulet considers his daughter as property, to trade or not to trade, as the "market" demands. Old Capulet, because of personal temperament and false assumptions, totally fails his daughter. At the same time, he brings about a situation that can only end with his daughter's death. Her growth into womanhood is seen in her refusal to remain an easily manipulated girl under her father's thumb. Capulet rages against her and threatens her when she staunchly disobeys him by refusing to marry Paris. In another rebellious step—the first being her marriage to Romeo— she leaves her father's house. Although hers and Romeo's deaths bring sorrow, their sires and elders characteristically continue to show their grief in "material terms."

One of the most painful scenes in Shakespeare is Lord Capulet's berating of Juliet. When I first read it, at Juliet's age, I felt only the scalding force of the father's rage—wave after wave of insults, threats, and curses. Without understanding what some of his words meant, I was all too clear about their tone: he hated her, his only child, to the point of wishing her dead.

And what had Juliet done to provoke this volcano? Said politely, that, at fourteen, she was not yet ready to marry—an

Sharon Hamilton, "The Father as Inept or Able Mentor: *Romeo and Juliet* and *The Tempest*," in *Shakespeare's Daughters*, Jefferson, NC: McFarland & Co., Inc., 2003, pp. 13–34. Copyright © 2003 Sharon Hamilton. All rights reserved. Reproduced by permission of McFarland & Company, Inc., Box 611, Jefferson NC 28640. www.mcfarlandpub.com.

opinion that Capulet himself had expressed to her suitor, the Count Paris, only two days earlier. I understood, too, the enormous gap between the reasons she was giving him and her actual predicament: secretly married to Romeo, the son of her family's great enemy, Juliet cannot obey her father's wishes without betraying the precepts of society and religion: bigamy is both a crime and a sin. Her private scruples are even more compelling. The timing of the confrontation is particularly cruel. Juliet has just consummated her marriage and bade her young husband a wrenching farewell. Romeo is making his way out of the Capulet orchard even as her parents enter her room. To so enamored a bride, the thought of admitting a second "husband" to her bed is repellent.

But Juliet never ventures to reveal her true situation to her father, and in that secrecy, too, my adolescent self identified with her. Who could expect such a tyrant to listen, much less sympathize? If Capulet is this furious at her request that he delay the marriage to Paris, what would he say to the news that she has made it impossible—and by marrying a Montague? Juliet is convinced that, to her father, she has done the unforgivable. I agreed with her completely: better to keep the secret, to remain true to Romeo and to her own integrity, even at the risk of death. At that point, I naively assumed that Shakespeare was Capulet, that the playwright was speaking through the enraged man. Only later did I realize that, of course, he was as much the daughter as the father, that he felt Juliet's hurt and fear and wrote the scene so that I would feel them, too.

A Father's Rage

The quarrel escalates to the point that Capulet issues Juliet a stark ultimatum: "An you be mine, I'll give you to my friend; / An you be not, hang, beg, starve, die in the streets" (III.v.193–94). This is the marriage mart, with the daughter as commodity. Either she agrees to be sold to the highest bidder or she loses all value. How have they come to this terrible impasse? What has happened to turn this child from the pride of her father's life to the object of his unmitigated fury?

From the beginning, Juliet, like [*The Tempest*'s] Miranda, is identified in the cast list through her relationship to her father: she is "daughter to Capulet." But in feud-torn Verona, "Capulet" is not simply a family name: it is a prescribed set of loyalties, an implied code of behavior. As the Prologue tells us, it is the "continuance of their parents' rage" that will prove fatal to the lovers. In fact, the first time that we see Lord Capulet, he is calling for his sword and claiming that he must wield it to counter "old Montague," who, he charges, "flourishes his blade in spite of me" (I.i.75–76). Choler and impulsiveness are his character notes. But as he later admits to Paris, that show of force was largely bluster: Keeping the peace, he confides, is no great burden for "men so old" as he. Toward his daughter, Capulet's rage knows no such limits.

The Montagues, in contrast, never show anger towards Romeo; in fact, they scrupulously avoid intruding on his privacy, even when he is causing them pain. Lord Montague is concerned about Romeo's "black and portentous humor" (I.i.139) and has "importuned" him to reveal the source of his melancholy. His motive is not idle curiosity but compassion. He assures Benvolio: "We would as willingly give cure as know" (I.i.153), and then leaves Romeo in peace to talk over his troubles with his friend. Whether because a son in this society is given more latitude or because they are naturally understanding, the Montagues grant Romeo trust and independence. Juliet's parents give her neither of these boons.

A Father's Pride

It is not that Capulet does not love Juliet: the play is his tragedy as well as hers. But he does not show that love in ways that benefit her. He is enormously proud of her grace and eloquence, but that very pride contains the seeds of her destruction, for it is largely the pride of ownership. Capulet himself would never put the case in such crass terms. He sees himself as the indulgent patriarch whose only concern is for his daughter's happiness. He plays that role when Paris first comes to pay court. Capulet refuses the eager suit by describing Juliet in tenderly protective terms: "My child is yet a stranger in this world," not yet "ripe to be a bride" (I.ii.8, 11). But almost at once he changes his mind, either because he does not want to put a damper on romance or because, as he later tells Juliet, this is too rich an offer to lose.

He feigns humility about Juliet's looks, advising the young count to compare her to the other ladies at the feast and "like her most whose merit most shall be" (I.ii.31). In fact, Capulet, cosmopolite and ladies' man, knows that Juliet is a striking beauty. The plot depends on the instantaneous passion she inspires in both Paris and Romeo. In spite of the father's qualms about her youth, he cannot resist showing her off and observing the young man's reactions. He gives Paris permission to "woo her," "get her heart." That done, he says, "My will to her consent is but a part" (I.ii.16–17). The rhyme suggests his complacent belief in this liberal attitude—as long as he can designate the suitor. Having approved of Paris's qualifications, he is ready to grant the girl freedom to second his choice.

At the play's outset, Juliet is too naive to oppose such a plan. She is the "lamb" and "ladybird" (I.iii.3) of the Nurse's pet names, a girl eager to please the parents who have indulged her. When her mother introduces the idea of marriage to Paris, Juliet responds politely to what for her is merely a theoretical situation: "It is an honor that I dream not of" (I.iii.66). Clearly, this is a subject that discomforts both mother and daughter. Lady Capulet was herself married very young—as she tells Juliet, she was only about fourteen when she bore *her*. Her husband is roughly twice her age. (At the ball he hosts, Capulet recalls dancing at a fete that occurred some thirty years before.) That early marriage "marred"

(I.ii.13) his wife, he hints to Paris, and certainly Lady Capulet seems stiff and repressed. The necessity of discussing sex with her pubescent daughter brings on waves of embarrassment, and Lady Capulet takes refuge in a formal tone and euphemistic phrasing. Since Juliet has never met Paris, the Lady describes his "beauty" in a series of conventional metaphors. He is a "flower," a "fair volume" unbound and awaiting a wife to provide a "cover" for the "golden story" of their love (I.iii.85–92). It takes the earthy Nurse, whom the awkward mother has invited to join the tête-à-tête, to undercut the pretty image with ribald candor. She reminds us—and Juliet—what conjugal love really entails: "happy nights" and, for the woman, "growing bigger" with child (I.iii.105, 95). Perhaps the discrepancy in the Capulets' ages accounts for the tension in their marriage, the resentful subjugation of wife to husband, and for the coldness of the mother toward her only child. Their experience of the harmful effects of premature marriage does not, however, dissuade either parent from urging Juliet's subjection to that fate.

Juliet is embarrassed, too, by both her mother's awkwardness and the delicacy of the subject. But she sees no objection to the plan and gives the Good Girl's answer that her mother is waiting to hear: She will "look to like," as her mother bids, but make no deeper commitment than "your consent" permits (I.iii.97–99). The "your" is plural: Juliet realizes that Lady Capulet is acting as her husband's emissary.

Falling in love with Romeo dashes the scales from Juliet's eyes and galvanizes her will. It makes her see beyond the petty enmity wrought by the feud. After she discovers the devastating fact that her new love is "Romeo, and a Montague," she wills him fancifully: "Deny thy father and refuse thy name" (II.ii.34). Unaware that he is eavesdropping on her "counsel," she maintains: "Thou art thyself, though not a Montague." She, in turn, offers to shed her old identity: "be but sworn my love, / And I'll no longer be a Capulet." Juliet also comes to understand the generosity essential to love, romantic and familial:

My bounty is as boundless as the
sea,

My love as deep; the more I give to
thee,

The more I have [II.ii.133–35]

The aim should be to give everything that will enhance the beloved's well being. The giving is its own reward. Juliet's father, for all his years and experience, is oblivious to those precepts.

Meanwhile, Capulet is pursuing his own scheme for Juliet's future. When Tybalt is killed, instead of delaying the marriage, the old Lord decides to hasten it. A practical man, he is not deeply grieved by his nephew's death: "Well, we were born to die" (III.ii.4), he says with facile stoicism. He is annoyed by the inconvenient timing, but agrees at first that Juliet must be granted one night, at least, to mourn her cousin. As Paris begins to take a respectful departure, however, Capulet suddenly disrupts the decorous arrangement. While before he argued with the ardent suitor that Juliet should be allowed two more years to mature, now he rashly accepts the proposal. He admits that he is making "a desperate tender / Of [his] child's love." But he adds immediately: "I think she will be ruled / In all respects by me; nay more, I doubt it not." The tentative claim has become a strident assertion. Lady Capulet's silence suggests that she is used to bending to her husband's will.

In Capulet's mind, Count Paris has all the qualifications— rank, wealth, and appearance:

A gentleman of noble parentage,

Of fair demesnes [domain], youthful, and nobly trained,

Stuffed, as they say, with honorable
parts. . . [III.v.181–83]

This suitor is a great bargain, a unique "tender" of "fortune" that Juliet—or rather Capulet—cannot refuse. Ironically, this description would fit Romeo as well as Paris, with the added advantage that the alliance could be the means of ending the pernicious feud. That, in fact, is Friar Laurence's avowed purpose for agreeing to perform the secret rite. Could Capulet heed his daughter's pleas, universal happiness would be the likely outcome.

Capulet has an inkling that Juliet will not welcome these hugger-mugger arrangements. The sign is that he goes into his Lord of the Manor mode, sending his wife on ahead to announce the decision, issued in a series of imperatives: "go you," "bid her," "a Thursday tell her / She shall be married to this noble earl" (III.iv.15–21). Lady Capulet recites to her daughter the official line: Juliet's "careful" father has arranged for her "a sudden day of joy" (III.v.108–09). Once Juliet has cut through the sugar coating and discovered the bitter facts, she protests vehemently to the haste of the match and asserts that she feels no attraction for the suitor she has met only once. Better be wed to Romeo, she tells her mother in a bold double entendre, "whom you know I hate." But Juliet's purported freedom of choice, so lately touted by each of her parents, is now only a memory. When she asks Lady Capulet to tell her "lord and father" that she does not wish to marry "yet," the mother washes her hands of the matter: "Tell him so yourself / And see how he will take it at your hands" (III.v.125–26). The sarcastic tone suggests that she has experienced before her husband's reaction to opposition.

Juliet tries in every way she can to tell her father—without telling him why—this marriage is repellent to her. Capulet notices that she is crying copiously, but he merely tries to tease her out of her sorrow. He has convinced himself that a little wedding cheer is just the thing to ease Juliet's grief, supposedly for Tybalt. When his witticisms fail, he returns to the purpose of the family conclave and demands: "How now, wife? / Have you delivered our decree?" (III.v.138–39). As his choice of words underlines, this is a command issued from on high. For response, he expects not only acquiescence but "thanks."

Juliet is well aware of his expectations, and she tries to balance candor about her true feelings with sensitivity to his wounded pride. When, at last, she refuses outright, he explodes. From his point of view, he has done everything possible to fulfill his paternal duty: all his "care," he claims melodramatically, "hath been to have her matched" (III.v.179–80). Not, it should be noted, married to one she loves but "matched" with a prestigious mate. In his frustration, Capulet loses all sense of proportion. He calls this supposedly beloved child a "wretched puling fool," "a whining mammet." He mocks her voice and her objections: "'I'll not wed, I cannot love; / I am too young, I pray you pardon me'" (III.v.187–88). The girl's pallor, caused by her sleepless wedding night and the shock of this crisis, evokes not pity but scorn: "you tallow-face!" "you green-sickness carrion!" he shouts. Even Lady Capulet is taken aback: "Fie, fie! Are you mad?" she protests. He admits, with an oath, the truth of her charge, though he lays the blame for his outburst on Juliet's refusal: "God's bread! it makes me mad" (III.v.177). He utters the terrible wish that "God" had never "lent" them "this only child," an ominous curse that echoes his wife's "I would the fool were married to her grave!" (III.v.141).

As his tantrum comes to a climax, Capulet puts his claim of ownership in the harshest terms: Juliet is either "his" to "give to [his] friend" or her own to "hang, beg, starve, die in the streets" (III.v.193–94). The hyperbolic verbs suggest how out of control he is: each one stabs. Some might argue that Capulet is no different from other fathers in Shakespeare's day: that he had not only the power but the duty to arrange his daughter's marriage. But the play does not support that reading. It criticizes the cruel manner in which he imposes his will, in the shocked protests of both Lady Capulet and the Nurse. More important, it shows the dire results of his treatment in Juliet's suicide. Shakespeare is no advocate for Capulet's embodiment of the paterfamilias.

In fairness, it must be conceded that Capulet has no idea of Juliet's real motives for refusing Paris's offer. She never confides in her parents, and he has no such magical device as [*The Tempest's*] Prospero's cloak for eavesdropping on her courtship. But neither does he have the magician's empathy. It is clear why Juliet feels driven back on her own small resources. When she tries to "beseech . . . on [her] knees" his "patience" to let her "speak but a word" (III.v.160–61), he silences her with a threat: "Speak not, reply not, do not answer me! My fingers itch." Some stagings of the scene have shown Capulet in fact striking his daughter. But such physical violence undercuts the emotional pain he is inflicting. A slap, frank and direct, might have been easier for her to bear than the scalding torrent of blame and abuse. Capulet's final pronouncement reveals the real basis for his rage: "I'll not be forsworn." He has given Paris his word as a gentleman. Maintaining his reputation as generous host and undisputed head of his clan means more to him than succoring his only child.

A Goal of Independence

Juliet, as the Chorus implies, has few "means" (II.Cho., 11) for breaking out of the strict course that her father has set her. She is either at home or at church, and she is subject to his rule. But she keeps striving for some control. After Capulet has stalked off, she turns to the parent who might still intercede in her behalf: "O sweet my mother, cast me not away!" It is the most intimate and piteous tone that Juliet has used toward her. She asks her only to "delay this marriage," and she concludes with a veiled threat of suicide: if she is forced, her "bridal bed" will be in Tybalt's "monument." But Lady Capulet is either too status-conscious or too afraid of her husband's temper to heed her: "Do as thou wilt, for I have done with thee," she says, and leaves the chamber. In her hour of greatest need, Juliet meets total rejection from both her parents.

When the Nurse, too, abandons her, Juliet is left in despair. Her last recourse is the Friar who performed the marriage ceremony. Before going to him, she makes a desperate vow: "If all else fail, myself have power to die." She has come to see suicide as her last means of asserting her will and remaining "a stainless wife" to Romeo. Rather than condemn this suicide wish as the ultimate sin, in accord with his vocation, the Friar commends her "strength of will" (IV.i.72). He proposes a course nearly as escapist and adolescent as Juliet's: that she take a potion that simulates death, awaken in the family vault, and run away with Romeo. He warns that the scheme requires enormous "valor" and that no "womanish fear" must deter her (IV.i.119–20). Never does Friar Laurence consider going to her parents with the truth and making a plea for this compelling reason to end the feud. Perhaps he, like Juliet, fears Lord Capulet's probable fury, a qualm that is justified by the outburst that we have just witnessed.

Juliet's desperation makes her welcome the feigned death that Friar Laurence proposes. With a brief, fervent prayer, "Love give me strength," she accepts the vial he offers. Her last words to him are affectionate and grateful: "Farewell, dear father." Imbibing the soporific acts as a kind of rehearsal for her actual suicide and makes it easier for Juliet to carry out her fatal resolve. Unlike Romeo, who at least sends his father a final letter, she has no words of farewell for her actual father. Could Juliet have awakened as her parents discover her supposed corpse, she would no doubt have been amazed at the intensity of their grief.

Capulet, for his part, does not take his rejection of Juliet seriously, as Shakespeare signals when he shifts the action to the father's point of view. In spite of the quarrel's rancor, the old lord has gone on happily planning the wedding. The news that Juliet has gone to Laurence's cell, supposedly to confess her wrongs, makes him jubilant. "He may chance to do her good," Capulet says condescendingly, and describes Juliet in tones of grumbling affection: "A peevish self-willed harlotry it is". His mood becomes positively buoyant when she returns "with merry look." His words to her are fond and teasing: "How now, my headstrong? Where have you been gadding?" On one level, he is proud of her show of temper, seeing in it a reflection of his own strong will. Juliet has learned the futility of revealing her true feelings. Instead, she assumes the persona of the Penitent Child, supposedly advocated by Friar Laurence. In her eagerness to try the Friar's dire remedy, she overplays the role. She will "fall prostrate," she says, and "beg [her father's] pardon." And she adds the cunning lie: "Henceforward, I am ever ruled by you". Capulet is entirely fooled: "This is well. . . . This is as't should be". He congratulates himself on his success as moral authority: "My heart is wondrous light, / Since this same wayward girl is so reclaimed". In his delight, he moves the wedding a fatal day forward, careless of the sleepless night and hasty preparations that the change entails.

The Father's Responsibility

Why does Juliet die? In a nutshell, because her father's own concept of her future makes him oblivious to hers. Seen from Capulet's perspective, his plan is not only reasonable but generous. He has found an ideal suitor for her, accepted the young man's proposal, and arranged a gala celebration in the couple's honor. When the girl unexpectedly refuses, claiming to be too young and too shocked by her cousin's death, he dismisses those pleas as callow. When Juliet persists, he throws the sort of tantrum that has always before allowed him to prevail. We have seen a minor instance of Capulet's temper in his squelching of Tybalt's own tantrum at the feast: "Am I the master here or you?" the old lord demanded. Ownership is authority. The girl is naturally shocked by the suddenness of the match, he reasons, so she cries and whines, but he refrains from striking her and waits for her to see her duty. Juliet returns from confession apparently persuaded that he is right. Capulet, elated, is convinced both that father knows best and that he has won, for himself and for her.

Juliet's sudden "death" knocks flat the whole self-flattering facade. Lord Capulet's reaction is more complex than his wife's and the Nurse's hysteria. Stunned, he begins not by lamenting the fact of Juliet's death but by describing its effect on her body in terms of almost scientific objectivity: "she's cold! / Her blood is settled, and her joints are stiff". Then, as the truth sinks in, Capulet goes through several stages of shock and grief. Juliet's beauty and youth come suddenly clear to him with a poignancy he never felt when he considered those qualities his to display. He is moved to mournful simile: "Death lies on her like an untimely frost / Upon the sweetest flower of all the field".

For a few moments, he is too overcome to speak further: "Death . . . ties up [his] tongue". With the entrance of Paris and the Friar, his poetic sentiments take a grotesque turn. Death becomes personified as his "son-in-law" and "heir," "deflowerer" of Juliet, "Flower as she was." Abruptly, Capulet realizes that his loss is final and absolute: "I will die / And leave him all. Life, living, all is Death's". He becomes more overwrought, first tenderly addressing the dead girl and then arriving at a more intimate understanding of the tragedy:

O child, o child! my soul, and not
my child!

Dead art thou—alack my child is
dead,

And with my child my joys are
buried [IV.v.62–64].

He has come finally to a realization so simple that he has never before acknowledged it: Juliet was uniquely precious, his only child, the person whose "soul" most resembled his own. With her have died any possibility of future encounters, any hope of replicating her features in a grandchild, any foreseeable happiness.

Capulet is moved not only to a full sense of his loss but, at last, to empathy for his daughter's anguish. The other mourners describe only the effects of the death on them, but he seems in addition to sense what Juliet suffered in her final hours, when she was "Despised, distressed, hated, martyred, killed." At the end, Paris still believes that Juliet died of "grief" over Tybalt's loss. Only when she is actually dead will the Friar reveal the "true ground of all these piteous woes"—that Lord Capulet "would have married her perforce."

Juliet is not faultless. She marries without her parents' consent and then keeps the act a secret. She never confides in them the real explanation for her angst and so gives them no chance to react, either to manifest their opposition or to overcome it. On the other hand, every approach that she makes to such confiding, every plea for understanding, meets with rejection. Admittedly, this is art, not life: the pace and circumstances of the lovers' crisis are more extreme than they would likely be in actuality. Still, in stylized form, the ways that feelings lead to actions ring true. People in general and adolescents in particular often only hint at their deepest hopes and fears. Those who care about them must listen for what they mean as well as what they say. Denial and coercion breed deception: Capulet drives Juliet to show him the image of herself that he has demanded to see. He discovers her actual plight—and her worth—only when it is too late.

Capulet understands the effect of the feud in causing the scourge on the families. He tells Montague that the lovers are "poor sacrifices of our enmity." As in *The Tempest*, the old enemies are reconciled by their children's love, though by partaking not in "wedding cheer" but "sad burial feast." The be-reaved fathers take refuge in the only consolation they can conceive: providing "statue[s] in pure gold" of their dead chil-dren. Capulet is oblivious to the irony that Juliet's "rate" is once again being expressed in material terms. How fully does he realize that even the "ancient grudge" would not have killed his daughter if he had listened with "patient ears" (first Chorus) to her soul's voice?

Maturation and Subversion

François Laroque

François Laroque is professor of English at the University of Paris, Sorbonne Nouvelle, and the author of Shakespeare's Festive World.

In the following essay, François Laroque argues that young love in Romeo and Juliet *subverts every aspect of established society, creating a fusion of discordant elements that, of itself, generates great energy. It undermines both social and political authority and questions the patriarchal order. The early Shakespeare loved showing the "ravages of misrule," he notes. Shakespeare furthermore presents multiple, clashing points of view, which adds to the play's force. Love, for example, subverts the establishment, but is, in turn, subverted by Mercutio's wit and the Nurse's bawdy realism. The play also undermines gender roles and the normal patterns of love and death. The old survive and the young die. In the final scene, the golden statue, which represents the "triumph of tradition over individual desire," actually represents disaster, the sacrifice that had to be made for this victory, the death of life-renewing forces: the young.*

*R*omeo and Juliet, the story of "star-crossed" love, is so well and so deeply rooted in a number of traditions—those of myth, legend, folklore, novella, to name a few—that to present it as a subversive play may appear paradoxical and perhaps even perverse. Yet the play's main polarities that explore the frictions between high and low spheres, public and private lives, age and youth, authority and rebellion, sacred and secular love, generate powerful whirls of energy that partly account for its enduring fascination for world audiences. . . .

François Laroque, "Tradition and Subversion in *Romeo and Juliet*," in *Shakespeare's "Romeo and Juliet": Texts, Contexts, and Interpretation*, ed. Jay L. Halio, Cranbury, NJ: University of Delaware Press, 1995, pp. 18–36. Copyright © 1995 by Associated University Presses, Inc. All rights reserved. Reproduced by permission.

Subversive Love

The law is subverted by a love that brings about a destabilization of domestic order, thus leading to a world where contraries are reconciled in a series of sublime or grotesque conjunctions (high and low, hate and love, the sacred and the profane, life and death) so as to create a series of discordant fusions. Shakespeare is here influenced by dramatist and poet [Christopher] Marlowe, whose heterodox [unorthodox] approach to life and love, repeatedly stressed in his plays, allowed the pagan mysteries to displace or subvert the traditional Christian values that were then regarded as the foundation of public order and of household peace.

Young Shakespeare seems to have delighted in delineating the ravages of misrule, of the hurly-burly of love and desire, in a traditional aristocratic society dominated by custom, patriarchy, and well established wealth. Festivity is not limited to orchestrating the coming of age in Verona or the various rites of passage for young men and women, but it also serves to turn the world upside down, subvert its rigid hierarchies. United with the subversive power of love, festivity does not only achieve a temporary suspension of social rules and political authority, but it also leads to a radical questioning of traditional patriarchal order. . . .

In the play's dialectics, love is a transcending force that disrupts and subverts the marriage strategies of the establishment but is itself subverted by Mercutio's wit and by the Nurse's bawdy humor. In creating a multiplicity of perspectives, Shakespeare is able to view the central love story from conflicting and parallel lines and thus deflate some of its potential pathos and sentimentality. . . .

Voices of Tradition

The voices of tradition and subversion are not one-sided in the play but constantly interact and reflect one another so that they oblige the spectator and the reader to resort to constant realignment of perspective. We find a similar dynamic at the level of social, sex, and gender roles, as well as of ideological positions in general.

That the Nurse should be regarded as one of the strong voices of tradition in the play seems an undeniable fact. In her long rambling speech about Juliet's age in 1.3 she seems to be the keeper of family memory, reminiscing numerous details about Juliet's infancy and growth to childhood—(her weaning, her standing "high lone," her falling forward). . . .

The subversion of the border between life and death at the initiative of figures that seem hallmarked by tradition and experience follows another subversion, namely that of gender roles in the play. . . .

Role Reversal

The love between the two children of enemy families leads to a reversal of ordinary social and sexual roles and to the subversion of the borders between life and death. The initial transgression lies in the love at first sight experienced during the masque at old Capulet's house, and it will subsequently defeat all the plans worked out by the traditional forces and voices of authority in the play (parents, confessor, Nurse). Paradoxically, the speeches that remind us of times past, of grave customs and ancient power, are laden with ironical foreboding of the inevitable transgression and subversion of tradition that will be allowed to take place. The subversion of life by death is itself an old idea found in morality plays, and it is mainly due to its being placed in a Renaissance context and applied to a pair of young and innocent lovers that it may be regarded as sensational or shocking. More intriguing is the ambiguous game played with the idea and the gruesome representation of death itself, which is responsible for the creation of horror with a sort of morbid . . . thrill. The repeated occurrences of the normally rather rare figure of the oxymoron serve [as Gayle Whittier notes] to "define the carnal knowledge of a love in which life and death intertwine" and this macabre representation is given pride of place, often with a highly visual emphasis, in important soliloquies. . . .

Tradition in *Romeo and Juliet* is certainly seen as a constraint that reduces the freedom of the individuals, obliging them to follow the inherited hatreds of the clannish feud, "the continuance of their parents' rage," as the sonnet Prologue puts it, rather than gratify their own inclinations. On the other hand, the importance or the precedence given to tradition also implies that there is an obligation inherent in ceremony, a respect due to the laws of hospitality that, for instance, leads Old Capulet to curb Tybalt's fury when he recognizes Romeo hiding behind his "antic face" in the ball scene.

But Shakespeare treats the whole relation in a more complex, dialectic manner, as tradition in the play combines order and disorder, discipline and disobedience (to the Prince and to the laws of Verona). Moreover, characters like the Nurse and the Friar, who represent the voices of tradition, engage in soliloquies full of subversive potential. Their various attitudes and actions in the play also favor the clandestine resistance of the lovers to their family traditions. Does not Friar Laurence, after all, go far beyond the allowed limits of the church tradition and of his own responsibility as a holy man when he tampers with the forces of life and death and allows Juliet to "continue two and forty hours" in a "borrow'd likeness of shrunk death". . . .

In the last analysis, their death is the sign of a triumph of sterility over the hope for continuity and regeneration, since it is not the old who die in the play, as tradition and natural laws would have it, but mainly the young (Mercutio, Tybalt, Paris, Romeo, and Juliet). The golden statues raised by the parents to commemorate the two eponymous heroes in the end are a sad and painful tribute, a mourning monument built to remind future generations of the dangers of civil strife and of the triumph of tradition over individual desire with its subversive potential. But, as the play itself plainly shows, this Pyrrhic victory is just another name for disaster since it is achieved at considerable expense, that of the sacrifice of the young and of the forces of life and renewal.

The Chaos and Violence of Coming of Age

Jill L. Levenson

Jill L. Levenson, professor of English at Trinity College of the University of Toronto, authored Romeo and Juliet *(2000) and edited* The Weakest Go to the Wall *(1980).*

In the following essay, Jill L. Levenson posits that Shakespeare, in dealing with the early and middle adolescence of his lovers, creates a sexually charged atmosphere of energy, action, and violence that has repercussions, throughout all phases of society in the play, threatening or challenging the patriarchal family and the patriarchal state, both of which act as tyrants. Violence and social disorder together become the driving force of the story. Weapons, along with people eager to use them, appear all through the drama—sometimes as props and sometimes as stage action. In addition, Levenson notes, the violence, which is shown determining all expression in the play itself, accurately reflects the reality of Elizabethan England. Romeo and Juliet cannot wholly break from the society in which they live, although they try. The feud is everything, until their deaths end it. Yet even in the end, Levenson writes, there are "no signs of lasting change."

By contrast, the dramatic version catches the lovers specifically in the early and middle phases of adolescence. Its portrayal of these phases, remarkable for its accuracy and thoroughness, is animated by sexual energy. When wordplay imitates sexual play, it expresses thoughts and sensations typical of this often chaotic period of transition. The staging itself charges events:

> Visually, the play remains memorable for a number of repeated images—street brawls, swords flashing to the hand,

torches rushing on and off, crowds gathering. The upper stage is used frequently, with many opportunities for leaping or scrambling or stretching up and down and much play between upper and lower areas. The dominant feelings we get as an audience are oppressive heat, sexual desire, a frequent whiz-bang exhilarating kinesthesia of speed and clash, and above all a feeling of the keeping-down and separation of highly charged bodies, whose pressure toward release and whose sudden discharge determine the rhythm of the play.

Perhaps the sexually charged enactment of adolescence explains the emotional appeal of *Romeo and Juliet* to modern teenagers and to adults still in touch with their earlier selves.

In its portrayal of adolescent phases, *Romeo and Juliet* uses the sequence of the well-known story as a point of departure. It adds scenes and shorter passages to the fictional narrative which enlarge the social worlds of the lovers before reducing them, and which therefore complicate relationships with families or friends. Consequently the changes of adolescence, part of a larger dynamic, set off repercussions at every level of the action: the protagonists verbalize them and act them out; Romeo's friends mirror or disagree with his behaviour; and the older generation, misconstruing almost all of the signs, hasten events towards calamity.

In the opening scene, for example, more than half of dialogue elaborates on Romeo's state of mind. When the prototype failed to rationalize his initial lovesickness in the novellas, an anonymous friend lectured him on the wastefulness of unrequited love, and Romeo immediately accepted his advice to find a more compassionate mistress. Revising this episode, the play makes Romeo's behaviour the subject of conversation between his father and his cousin Benvolio: Romeo isolates himself, restless and uncommunicative, seeking an ambience that suits his mood. Benvolio not only shares some of Romeo's feelings (ll.114–26) but recognizes the correspondence:

> I, measuring his affections by my
> own . . .
>
> Pursued my humour, not pursuing
> his,
>
> And gladly shunned who gladly
> fled from me.
>
> (ll.122–6)

Yet neither relative can identify Romeo's problem, an obvious case of unsettled hormones, and Benvolio determines to help Montague find the cause. . . .

Patriarchy, the system which licenses individual men of power to transfer their authority to other individual men, had already added historical dimensions to the novellas. In the drama it is more of a presence, filling all the public space and intruding, on privacy as well, not only in the family but in the subjective experience of individuals. Some of its most prominent features match current realities more exactly than they do in the sources, making the play immediate and critical.

Extended in these ways, the feud allows the narrative to draw correspondences between patriarchal state and patriarchal family, political and social order. Prince Escalus attempts to regulate his city, Capulet his family, and both fail because of conflicts within the system. In the early modern era, this juxtaposition contributed more to the play than symmetry. It set unpredictable state against predictable family; eruptive Verona against an established household; forms subject to change—political, economic, cultural—against 'old-accustomed' forms (1.2.20). Finally the most stable unit of the larger community cannot avoid the stresses inherent in the ideology, but it endures, and Verona endures. Only the younger generation, who internalize imperatives of the feud in the process of becoming adults, pay the ultimate price for its unreasonable demands. The play depicts their crisis in contemporary terms, heightening correspondences in the fiction with analogies from Elizabethan life.

In the earliest texts of *Romeo and Juliet*, unlawful violence is the most obvious sign of pressure within the system as a whole. As Derek Cohen says, writing about other Shakespearian plays, '[a]cts of violence belong to patriarchy as surely as fathers do'.

> They appear ... to issue directly from that system, indeed, are often logical, rational products of it. . . . Violence, both criminal and legitimate, is an essential form of cultural expression though it is always the dominant culture within society which gets to define criminality and legitimacy. For this reason acts of violence are all political in that they are absorbed by and conform to and, additionally, are produced by a social code which valorizes order as a social value.

Violence in *Romeo and Juliet*, generally unauthorized, not only facilitates the mechanics of plot but adds political implications. At the centre of each novella one dangerous confrontation had occurred: the brawl between Montagues and Capulets that leads to Romeo's banishment. Shakespeare invents two more conflicts, the row in 1.1 and the duel in 5.3, producing a narrative driven by social disorder through violence. Like the ideology in which they originate, the signs are pervasive.

Always ready for armed conflict, weapons appear everywhere in *Romeo and Juliet*. They range from current to obsolete—the rapiers of young gentlemen to the long sword of old Capulet—giving the familiar story new menace as well as concrete signifiers. Repeatedly the text calls for weapons as props; often the props make emblematic comments on the action. In the first scene Prince Escalus commands, 'Throw your mistempered weapons to the ground' (1.1.83), and they lie on the stage in disarray for Romeo to notice soon after he enters (1.1.169). In the last scene Friar Laurence finds the 'masterless and gory swords' dropped by Paris and Romeo (5.3.142), and

Capulet discovers Romeo's dagger 'mis-sheathed in my daughter's bosom' (l. 205). The text seems to require all of the male characters, except Friar Laurence, to wear weapons or have ready access to them; it reflects Elizabethan practice. At the Capulet ball Tybalt, outraged by Romeo's presence, orders his page, 'Fetch me my rapier, boy' (1.4.168), on the day after the feast Peter neglects to defend the Nurse with the weapon he carries (2.3.146–9). Friar Laurence, like the Apothecary, has poison at hand (2.2.23–4), Capulet's Wife plans to order some (3.5.88–91).

Weapons and fighting occur not only in the play's action but in the dialogue. As a topic of conversation they open the exchange between Samson and Gregory, a conversation that will be echoed later by Peter and the Musicians at the end of 4.4. They distinguish Mercutio's speeches: his fantasy of Queen Mab includes the soldier who dreams 'of cutting foreign throats, / Of breaches, ambuscados, Spanish blades' (1.4.81–2); his characterization of Tybalt portrays a duellist in the Spanish style. . . .

Mercutio's caricature of Benvolio as a quarreller trivializes the causes for which gentlemen fight: 'Thou hast quarrelled with a man for coughing in the street, because he hath wakened thy dog that hath lain asleep in the sun' (3.1.23–6). . . .

Charged with its ideology, violence determines all forms of expression in Verona, from public conversations to dress to the vocabulary of desire. It spans generations, and it infiltrates the love-story through both incident and verbal style. In the late sixteenth century it gained immediacy from the current events it reflected: violence was an intransigent reality in early modern England. Proclamations against fighting in public had been issued by Henry VII, Henry VIII, and Elizabeth. Despite these and other measures, civil disorder erupted in town and countryside until the turn of the century: brawls disturbed Fleet Street and the Strand; dangerous feuds threatened the peace of whole counties. As the Tudors attempted to contain

Still scene from the 1968 film version of Romeo and Juliet *with Michael York as Tybalt and John McEnery as Mercutio.* The Kobal Collection/The Picture Desk, Inc.

the capacity for violence, and therefore the power, of the aristocracy, infractions continued to escape them. By the 1590s Queen Elizabeth's policies were beginning to take hold, defusing violence through litigation or limiting it to private confrontation in duels, but street outbreaks persisted and the number of recorded duels and challenges jumped from five in the 1580s to nearly twenty in this decade [1590s]. With its feud, street fight, duelling, casualties, and deployment of combat imagery, *Romeo and Juliet* offers a panoramic view of violence in Elizabethan England.

Violence in all of its manifestations urgently signals disruptions in the patriarchal state of Verona: 'civil blood makes civil hands unclean' (Prologue 4); unlawful outbreaks betray a faltering system which cannot enforce regulations distinguishing criminality from legitimacy. With less force it makes a similar point about the patriarchal family, bound to the state in the play and in fact. What Natalie Zemon Davis writes about the patriarchal family from the sixteenth century to the eighteenth applies to Capulet's situation: 'In the little world of the family, with its conspicuous tension between intimacy and power, the larger matters of political and social order could find ready symbolization.'

From the first scene violence intrudes on Capulet's household, calling him from it on a Sunday morning as he responds to Montague, armed and also drawn from his home, by demanding his long sword. Soon violence will intrude on Capulet's marriage negotiations with Paris: their first exchange about Paris's suit in 1.2 follows Capulet's allusion to the feud and the Prince's efforts to suppress it; the festivities for viewing Juliet in 1.4 are threatened by Tybalt's fury over Romeo's appearance; and the wedding plans in 3.4 and the fourth act go awry, as far as Capulet knows, with the death of Tybalt. Of course these disturbances are superficial, little tremors from a deep cataclysm. With Juliet's defection and its terrible consequences Capulet loses his grip, more visibly than Montague, on his authority as a patriarch. . . .

The lovers cannot change or break their social constraints because they have so completely internalized them. However far they escape from gender norms—Juliet in manly risk-taking, Romeo in conciliatory gestures—circumstances force them to return: Juliet reaches a hallucinatory state verging on hysteria before she takes the sleeping potion; Romeo commits murder once in revenge, twice in fury. Nor can they escape their identities as members of rival houses. Everything's in a name, a genealogical marker of an individual's public and private history.

Dympna C. Callaghan describes *Romeo and Juliet* as a 'lyrical document of universal love' which stands within history 'doing the work of culture, instigating and perpetuating the production of socially necessary formations of desire.' Whether or not the play accomplishes such work, it certainly records its own cultural era with its contradictions and defaults. In this sense it shows adult society trying to ward off anomie while a young generation invites it, adapting a compromised ideology in the fervour to become individuals. Adolescent impatience and unreasonableness, keynotes of Mercutio and Tybalt in particular, encapsulate the feud, from its rivalries for power to its allegiances and poignancy. If Romeo and Juliet resist their socialization and for several fleeting days create a private world apart from Verona, they nevertheless continue to incorporate the familiar in the new, and they struggle to reconcile the new with the familiar. The play depicts them as vulnerable young lovers, fragile embodiments of ideas and values that test the status quo. In the coda to their deaths it qualifies their achievement. Their fathers celebrate the marriage with equally valuable gold-plated figures; Capulet regards the lovers as '[p]oor sacrifices of our enmity' (5.3.304). A melancholy spectacle, the tragedy brings '[a] glooming peace' (l. 305)—hardly new in Verona—but no signs of lasting change.

Social Issues
in Literature

CHAPTER 3

Contemporary
Perspectives on
Coming of Age

Young Love in the Twenty-First Century

Katherine Gazella

Katherine Gazella, a staff writer for Florida's St. Petersburg Times, *wrote a series for the paper about young love from which this excerpt is taken. She has also written, among other stories, about adolescents trying to kick heroin addiction, teenage suicide, and communes.*

Unlike the relationship in Romeo and Juliet, *this account of young love in the twenty-first century is not serious, tragic, intimate, or hidden. Instead, Katherine Gazella explores the ease of one young couple as they interact with each other and their friends.*

They sit shoulder to shoulder in the back of the white Mercury minivan, her neatly manicured right hand locked in his left. Mike throws a stuffed monkey at Jessica with his free hand; she catches it with hers and whips it back. They won't let go of each other, not even to fight.

Like Kids

The moment is sweet but hardly intimate. In the middle seat, Mike's 9-year-old brother, D.J., and his friend Andrew cackle loudly and spray each other with imaginary machine guns. You can always count on a kid brother to destroy a romantic moment.

Mike's dad is behind the wheel, good-naturedly performing his duties as chauffeur. He is driving the couple to Steak 'n Shake in Clearwater, where Mike and Jessica will sip milk shakes and Mike will steal strips of chicken from Jessica's plate and Jessica will gently stab Mike's hand with a fork. The last time they were there, they caught Mike's dad standing outside the restaurant, spying on them through the windows.

Let him look. Jessica Replogle, 14, and Mike Sharkey, 13, are in love, and they don't care who sees it—which is a good thing, because they are hardly ever alone. Theirs is a roller-rink-and-Gummi-bear romance. They talk on the phone for hours. He's slender and athletic, so naturally she calls him Chubby. They celebrate an anniversary every month. In classes at Safety Harbor Middle School, he writes her notes that begin, "Hey, Beautiful." She wears a charm necklace, a gift from him. "Taken," says the charm. (Should they ever break up, Mike jokes, he'll give her another charm: "Available.")

Jessica and Mike love being together and being in love.

Perfect but Not Forever

On this day in the minivan, they have been going out—dating each other exclusively—for precisely four months and nine days, a fact Jessica has at her exquisitely decorated fingertips. It is an endurance record for each of them.

"Things are, like, perfect right now," Jessica says.

How many people can say that about their relationships?

But like any romance between eighth graders, this one is fragile and probably fleeting. Perfect things often are. When we began working on this article, we met an eighth-grade girl from New Tampa who said oh, yes, she and her boyfriend would just love to tell us their story. But when we called to set up the interview, she made an excuse and backed out. Her mother later explained why. Ten minutes before we talked to her, the boy dumped her.

Mike has no such plans; he's smitten. Still, if we want to understand where love begins, we need to watch Mike and Jessica now, in this pristine moment.

At last the van arrives at Steak 'n Shake. When it stops, Mike bolts out so he can open the restaurant door for Jessica, an act of chivalry she has come to expect from him. Their love is one of the sweetest and most uncomplicated they will ever know.

True but "Lite" Love

The list of perfect things in the relationship includes Mike's tucked-in shirt.

It is Monday afternoon and Mike and Jessica are in his bedroom getting ready for a date. The time they will spend here provides a clear picture of the relationship, right down to the banter about Mike's shirt.

Mike, a snazzy dresser who sometimes changes his clothes three times in a day, twists and turns in front of the bathroom mirror, looking from all angles at the plaid button-down shirt he just put on. He pulls it out of his jeans a little in front, tucks it in a little more in back, checks the mirror again.

Mike is seeking what he calls The Perfect Tuck.

"It takes him, like, an hour to do," Jessica sighs. While she waits, she obsesses over a few details of her own appearance. She flattens her red shirt against her small waist, glosses her lips and brushes her long, middle-parted, blond-streaked hair.

Finally, Mike puts the finishing touches on the tuck of the century.

"Jessica, do I have it?" Mike asks, holding his arms up like a gymnast after a dismount.

"Nope," she says, then fixes one part of the shirt that was uneven. "There."

In some ways, Jessica and Mike are like an old married-couple; they know each other's bad habits and quirks. It drives her crazy when he twitches his knee. He jabs her in the side when she says "like," which is often. And she knows that even if she tells him to wait for her call, he will grow impatient and call her first.

"And have you seen his wall of hair?" Jessica says, poking her finger into his heavily-gelled 'do.

They gained this knowledge by spending a lot of time together. They meet in the hallway after fifth period when she's leaving math and he's coming out of language. They study together after school. They attend school basketball games together—Mike as a point guard, Jessica as a cheerleader. Go, Warriors.

At night they talk on the phone for hours at a time, but none of the conversations goes too deep. They usually end these marathons with a debate: "I love you more," she'll say. "No, I love you more," and so on.

They're like an old married couple, yes, but without the lingering resentments, the deep affection, the cycles of pain and forgiveness. Their love is true but it's also lite.

And they know it. When they are out with friends, as they will be today, Jessica will playfully drape her arm around another boy's shoulders and Mike will hug other girls.

"We'll both flirt with other people," Jessica says. "I mean, we're going out. We're not dead."

Love Among Friends

It is Jessica's 14th birthday, and 60—that is not a typo—of her closest friends are jammed into her living room for a party. These are the children of the mid-'80s, Generation Y. They wear hair scrunchies on their wrists and platform sneakers and low-slung Tommy Hilfiger jeans. Their names are Meghan and Tyson and Justin and Kalyn.

They're a peculiar subspecies, 14-year-olds; somehow, they're both children and adults, yet neither children nor adults. Theirs is a world of love notes passed in the hallways at school and i's dotted with hearts. It is also a world of skimpy tank tops, provocative songs, sexual exploration and sultry dancing.

You can see some of that right here, in Jessica's living room. Everywhere you look, kids are grinding their skinny hips to techno music. On a makeshift stage in the corner, other kids sing along to the music of a rented karaoke machine, appearing free of all inhibitions as they perform.

"Oooh! Me so horny," they sing.

At the same time, Winnie the Pooh and Rugrats balloons drift side to side, as if they, too, are trying to keep the beat.

One girl goes into the kitchen, her arms folded across her chest, and asks Jessica's mom to turn off the black light. One of the boys has announced that he can see her bra through her black sweater.

It's unlikely that any couple here has been dating more than a year, and chances are none will be together a year from now. And yet the songs they sing are all about grown-up romance, with all its passion and peril. On the karaoke stage, Jessica and eight other girls line up for one of the big numbers of the night.

"At first I was afraid, I was petrified," they sing.

The song is *I Will Survive*, the anthem of women's heartache and resilience. The girls belt out these words with dramatic flair, squinting to demonstrate pain, shouting loudly to portray passion.

Jessica's mom, Beverly, smiles as she watches. She's 42 and surprisingly calm amid all these boisterous teenagers. Five years ago she and Jessica's father were divorced—for the second time. She doesn't want to discuss it.

On stage, Jessica and the girls are still shouting out their song. "I'm trying hard to mend the pieces of my broken heart," they sing. One girl places her right hand over her heart, which is doubtless as pink and tender as filet mignon.

"They have no idea," Beverly says.

A portrait of a young couple in love. Image copyright Yuri Arcurs, 2009. Used under license from Shutterstock.com.

Save the Last Dance for Me

One of the kids keeps turning the light on and off, on and off, until finally someone tells him to stop it and the room goes dark.

"Ladies' choice!" one of the girls shouts. Most of the ladies choose to giggle and look at their shoes, too coy or bashful to ask a boy to dance. One girl pulls a girlfriend into the corner and, in a whisper, asks whether she should approach the boy she likes.

But Jessica is not shy or uncertain, and just a few notes into the Aaliyah song *One in a Million* she makes her move. She walks over to Mike and playfully butts her head into his chest. He grins, folds his arms around her waist and whispers something only she can hear.

Aaliyah sings:

Your love is a one in a million It goes on and on and on

Several couples join them on the carpeted dance floor. Many of the girls tower over their partners, their arms slanting downward to rest on the boys' shoulders.

But this is not the case for Jessica and Mike. She is three inches shorter than he is, the perfect height for dancing in the way long favored by teenagers: Her arms clasped behind his neck, his behind her waist, leaving no airspace between them. They shuffle side to side, hugging more than dancing, careful not to step on each other's bare feet.

Won't let no one come and take your place
Cuz the love you give can't be replaced.

Childhood Cut Short: The Arranged Marriages of Underaged Girls

Stephen Singular

Stephen Singular is an author, journalist, and television commentator. His books include Presumed Guilty *and* Unholy Messenger.

In the following article, Stephen Singular focuses on arranged and sometimes forced marriages as they occurred in the polygamous sect the Fundamental Latter Day Saints (FLDS). One fourteen-year-old (very much like Juliet) describes her strenuous objection when she finds she will have no choice in her fate. She approached each of the male leaders in the sect and was misled into believing that they would respect her wishes. (She would eventually be forced into the marriage but would subsequently accuse "The Prophet" of rape in court, a charge of which he was found guilty.)

By 2000, Warren Jeffs was in the awkward position of impatiently waiting for his father to die, while trying to appear reverent toward [his father] Rulon. The old man had faded so badly that he couldn't monitor everything his son did, and Warren had begun speaking for the Prophet about ridding the FLDS of enemies and apostates, laying the foundation for his coming reign. On July 17 of that year, at the LJS Meetinghouse in Hildale [Utah], he seemed to represent his father, who waited in the wings as Warren addressed the congregation:

I ask Heavenly Father to strengthen me at this time to deliver the message our Prophet has directed we receive this day . . . Let there be a separation of this Priesthood people from associations, business, and doings with apostates . . . An apostate . . . is the most dark person on earth. They are a liar from the beginning. They have made covenants to abide the laws of God and have turned traitor to the Priesthood and their own existence, and they are led about by their master, Lucifer . . .

And if you are choosing to socialize with apostates, to join with them in any way, you are choosing to get on the devil's ground . . . Stop patronizing businesses of the apostates . . . If you are in partnership with apostates, come away from them is the call of our Prophet, for your labors of earning money is strengthening their hand against this Priesthood . . .

Echoing Brigham Young's entries from 1876, Jeffs said, "The great challenge among this people is the apostates who are our relatives. If a mother has apostate children, her emotions won't let her give them up and she invites them into the home, thus desecrating that dedicated home . . .

Your only real family are the members of this Priesthood who are faithful to our Prophet . . . If any among this people work in a job for an apostate, he wants you to find a different job."

After Warren finished, his father commended him on the excellence of his sermon and repeated the same sentiments.

"Apostates," Rulon said from the pulpit, "have ingratiated themselves with their friendly relatives and it is poison. So let us separate ourselves and stand with the true cause of God and the Priesthood. It is all the way or nothing at all . . . So take this counsel that I have asked Brother Warren to deliver to this people today. God bless you. I pray in the name of Jesus Christ, amen."

In August 2000, Warren ordered all FLDS parents to pull their boys and girls out of the public schools serving Colorado City and Hildale, ending the children's interaction with gentile teachers and classmates who came from nearby Centennial Park. Enrollment at Phelps Elementary School dropped from 350 to 16. Washington County (Utah) eventually closed Phelps. The FLDS community tried homeschooling, but when it became too burdensome, the families organized more formal private schools. One was the Jeffs Academy, which moved into Phelps after the district sold it to the Twin Cities Improvement Association for pennies on the dollar. The result of all these changes was that local children were more isolated from the outside world and fell further and further behind in their education.

Jeffs and Underage Marriage

Another institution was coming under Warrens control as well, he was exercising it far from The Crick [referring to the small village that is on the border of Arizona and Utah].

The 160-mile drive from Colorado City to Caliente, Nevada, winds along the two-lane Route 56, leading through Utah's Antelope Mountains and across the Escalante Valley. By 2001, Nevada had become the best choice for FLDS wedding ceremonies, as Utah and Arizona authorities were finally stirring from their decades-long indifference to underage marriage. That year Utah Attorney General Mark Shurtleff had prosecuted one of the state's most notorious polygamists, Tom Green, who'd openly flaunted his lifestyle by claiming that he had five wives and twenty-nine children. Green was convicted of child rape for having sex with his first wife when she was thirteen. His legal troubles had widespread implications. They motivated pro-polygamy female activists—led by Marianne Watson, Mary Batchelor, and Anne Wilde—to form the advocacy group Principle Voices and to start networking with other Mormon fundamentalist women. Their mission included telling the media that they did not condone underage or arranged marriages, but that for consenting adults plural marriage could be a healthy choice. They also recommended that everybody should be at least eighteen before entering into wedlock.

Warren had followed the Tom Green case and decided that the border towns were no longer a safe haven for performing "celestial marriages." The isolated Caliente Hot Springs Motel in eastern Nevada was not only owned by church members, but was tucked far enough away to be safe from Utah and Arizona law enforcement.

Room 15 had no pews, arbors, pipe organ, or candlelabra, only a plain wooden dresser, bed, table, and soft. The motel featured therapeutic waters for people in search of healing or relaxation, but those traveling in caravans from Colorado City to Caliente for as many as ten weddings back-to-back were too busy to think about soaking in the hot springs. On weekends, they arrived as a pack and waited until most of the other guests had checked out of the motel or left for the day so strangers wouldn't see what they were doing. The brides usually came with their mothers or fathers, while the grooms brought along a few of their plural wives. During the ceremony, one of the wives usually held the bride's hand and placed it in the groom's, as a way of accepting her into the new family as a "sister wife."

An Arranged Marriage

In the spring of 2001, a fourteen-year-old girl named Elissa Wall was living in the Hildale home of ninety-year-old Fred Jessop, a bishop and the third-in-command inside the FLDS behind Rulon and Warren Jeffs. Elissa had grown up near Salt Lake City and attended Alta Academy before her family was broken up because of her father's behavioral problems. The church leadership decided he needed an "adjustment," and he was sent away. Elissa, her mother, Sharon, and her sisters were "reassigned" and moved in with the Jessops in Hildale. As a child, Elissa had spent time on a farm in southern Utah and gotten to know one of her first cousins, Allen Steed. Elissa had several pretty sisters and was attractive herself, with pink cheeks, long flowing blond hair, and an innocent smile, but she'd always been a little overweight and self-conscious about it. Allen criticized her appearance, calling her "Tubby Tuba" and other hurtful things. One time he shot Elissa with a hose filled with cold water, and she never forgot how it felt. To her, Allen was a mean-spirited bully.

The home Elissa's family moved into was vast, with forty bedrooms and half as many baths. Fred Jessop needed a lot of space to accommodate his fifteen or so wives and the three or four dozen others who lived there—after Elissa's mother came to stay with the old man, he married *her*. One April evening, Fred approached Elissa and mentioned that the Prophet "had a place" for his girls now, code language meaning that some of the local teenagers were about to be wed. FLDS girls had been taught at Alta, at home, and at church services that being selected as a marriage partner was the highest honor they could hope for. And then to have lots of children.

"There is no greater goal," they were told, "than to be a mother in Zion."

Fred looked surprised when Elissa didn't seem happy about this news. In fact, she didn't respond at all—assuming that he was talking about other girls in the community and not her. He repeated himself and this time made his message more clear: the Prophet had chosen a place for her.

Even as the words sunk in, she wasn't certain that Fred was serious.

A Young Girl's Rebellion

"I don't feel," the ninth-grader told the ninety-year-old, "this is what I should be doing."

He calmly nodded and suggested she go into her room and pray about her situation.

"Who am I supposed to marry?" she asked, but the old man refused to give her an answer.

After thinking about what Fred had told her and praying for a couple of days, she went back to him and said that she definitely wasn't ready for all the responsibilities of being a wife. The bishop listened patiently and then told her to go speak to the Prophet.

She phoned Rulon's compound and reached Warren, explaining that she was too young to get married and wanted to ask his father for advice. Warren also told her to pray about her situation, and said that he'd soon let Fred know what the plan was. Later that week, Warren contacted Jessop and said that God had called Elissa to be married now. When Fred conveyed this to the girl, she was stunned, but didn't express her feelings or argue with him. Since the first grade at Alta, she'd been taught that the Prophet was not just the church leader but God on earth and whatever he said wasn't just his opinion, but a direct command from the Lord. Still, she doubted she'd be forced into marriage at fourteen.

One spring night at a family gathering in the Jessop home, she was sitting next to her mother, and on her other side was an empty chair. Other women kept walking by and asking if she was excited about her upcoming wedding but she didn't know what to say. No spouse had been chosen for her and, in her mind at least, the matter seemed to be fading. Looking around the room she spotted her first cousin, Allen, who walked over and sat down beside her. Her mind suddenly clicked—this was the young man they'd selected as her husband! He wasn't just a close relative whom she disliked, but a bully.

Her cheeks flushed a deep shade of pink as she jumped up and hurried away.

Elissa ran into her mother's bedroom, lay down on the pillows, and began to sob.

Her mother came in and sat next to her.

"I can't marry him!" the girl said. "He's my first cousin! I won't do this."

Talk to Fred, Sharon told her in a reassuring voice. He'll know what is right. Just go talk to Fred.

The Leadership's Choice

When she confronted the old man and said that she could never be wife to Allen, he spelled out to her that this was how things worked in the FLDS and that she needed to understand and accept that. Uncle Rulon had ordered the wedding because it was the fulfillment of God's will. Elissa just needed to settle down and offer the Lord more prayers for her good fortune.

"You wouldn't defy what the Prophet wants, would you?" he asked.

"No," she replied. "No, I wouldn't. I just don't want to marry *him*."

Uncle Fred was taken aback. Why would a young woman being given the chance to enter into a good marriage be so distaught? This wasn't the way things had been done in the past, when teenage girls in the church had said yes to their weddings and made far more of an effort to keep sweet. Fred was so bewildered that he told Elissa to go back to the Prophet and seek his counsel again.

She called Warren and made an appointment to see his father, but when she arrived at the Jeffs's compound, the younger man spoke to her alone in Rulon's office. She tried to explain that she needed time to grow up before becoming someone's wife, but Warren gazed at her with a confused expression just as Fred had done.

Why, he asked her, would she or any other girl in the congregation not be thrilled to be getting married? This would give her a lifetime of security and respect within the church and the community. It was a great privilege to be joined with somebody from one of the more prominent FLDS families, and to receive the protection and support of her husband.

"Have you prayed about this?" Warren said.

"Yes, I have," the girl answered. "Many times. Everything inside of me is telling me not to do this."

Didn't she understand that the Prophet had received a revelation from God about her marriage to Allen?

She didn't know how to respond to his question, so they stared at one another across Rulon's desk.

"I need to hear it from the Prophet," she said.

Warren took her into the dining room, where his father was eating lunch with several of his wives. As the younger women hovered around the elderly man, Elissa knelt down at the Prophet's knee and said what a wonderful honor it was for her to be allowed near him. Surely, he would listen to her.

With his broad face and white hair sweeping back from his wide forehead, Rulon smiled at her gently.

"What can I do for you, sweetie?" he asked.

"I'm not trying to defy God's word," she said, "but I want to wait two years before I get married. Just two years."

The old man gave her the same perplexed expression Fred and Warren had. Why was she acting this way?

He didn't seem to know what to say.

"If I can't wait two years," she told him, "I can never marry Allen. Maybe someone else."

Rulon leaned in closer and cupped his ear.

"Sweetheart," he said, "I can't hear you. Can you repeat that?"

Elissa glanced up at Warren, who slowly explained to his father that the girl didn't want to marry her first cousin.

Rulon reached down and patted Elissa's hand.

"Follow your heart, sweetie." he said. "Just follow your heart." . . .

"My heart has told me that this marriage is all wrong."

"Your heart," Warren said softly, "is in the wrong place."

She stared at him in disbelief. Hadnt he heard what Rulon had just told her?

"But the Prophet—"

Raising his long thin hand, he cut her off and bluntly said that she needed to proceed with her wedding plans.

She was too stunned to argue.

Youthful Suicides

Dani Garavelli

Dani Garavelli, a journalist for Scotland on Sunday, *has written numerous articles on the problems of young people as well as on other current issues.*

In February 2008, in a small Welsh town, a twenty-year-old woman committed suicide after learning that her fifteen-year-old close friend and cousin had critically injured himself—what Dani Garavelli in the following article describes as "self harming." Shocking as this was, the event was made all the more appalling because it was the sixteenth suicide by hanging in the town within the year. All of the deaths were of young people between the ages of sixteen and twenty-seven. Garavelli explains that some investigators believe the deaths are connected to social networking sites frequented by a majority of the suicide victims. The isolation and alternative reality offered by the computer, as well as the potential for "imitative" suicides provoked by online memorials, are blamed for some deaths. Others argue that there have been epidemics of imitative youthful suicides throughout history. They generally occur in small, isolated towns and in closed communities such as jails, hospitals, and schools.

It was the news the people of Bridgend least wanted to hear. In a town where suicide seems to be spreading like a contagion, two more young people had taken their own lives within hours of each other.

Kelly Stephenson, 20, was found dead in a locked room on holiday in Kent on Valentine's Day. She had just been told her cousin Nathaniel Pritchard, 15, was critically ill in hospital after "self-harming" and was unlikely to pull through. Pritchard died on Friday, when his life support machine was turned off. The pair lived just 14 houses from one another and were said to be "very close".

They seemed to have everything to live for. On her Bebo site, Stephenson, who called herself Baby-Girl-Kelly, says: "I just love to live life to the full. Always up 4 a laugh and I don't like takin things too serious," although she did admit her greatest fear was losing those she loved. A keen footballer, she had just signed for Porthcawl Lightning Strikers [a soccer league].

Pritchard, too, seemed to have plenty of friends around him.

Epidemic Suicides

Their deaths—just a week after 18-year old Angeline Fuller killed herself—bring the grim toll of young suicide victims in Bridgend to 16 in the last year [2007–2008]. All were aged between 16 and 27 and all hanged themselves.

The scale of the deaths, and the similarity in their execution, has sparked panic in the 40,000 strong town.

Terrified of fuelling the phenomenon, those in authority have increasingly sought to deny any link between the deaths. Both Mark Walters, coroner for Bridgend and the Glamorgan Valleys, and South Wales Police have played down the notion that the spate is any more than a freak coincidence.

Campaigners, too, have lowered the shutters in the face of the tragedy, with the suicide prevention charity Papyrus going so far as to urge newspapers to stop reporting the deaths.

Yet, it takes an act of supreme will to see such a high number of suicides in such a short space of time as anything other than a sign that something is seriously amiss in the Welsh town.

Although there is no common denominator connecting the 16 people who have taken their own lives, most have been a friend or acquaintance of at least one of the previous victims. Stephenson, for example, knew both Gareth Morgan, 27, and Liam Clarke, 20, who hanged themselves last year [2007].

Responsibility of Networking Sites

Equally disturbingly, a large number of them belonged to social networking sites such as Bebo or Facebook on which news of each suicide has spread like wildfire.

Within hours of Pritchard's death, messages such as "What happened m8? Going to miss you. Cannot believe what has happened. There is no better place for you than down here. But I will no now that u r safer up there m8. Sleep tight" had been posted to his site.

After some of the suicides, remembrance walls made up of virtual bricks were erected on dedicated sites, leading some to speculate that the thought of securing "virtual immortality" was driving some of these vulnerable young people to take their own lives.

Bridgend MP [member of Parliament] Madeleine Moon is not one of those who wants the deaths to be played down, although she would prefer it if they were reported in less sensational terms. But she believes her constituency is like a microcosm of Wales at large, where the suicide rate has been disproportionately high for many years.

"This is not the time for delay," she has said. "This is the time for action. I do not want to be talking to journalists about further deaths. [I] want to talk about success and how wonderful Bridgend and Wales are to live, to work and raise a family in."

There is nothing in particular about Bridgend that marks it out as likely to have more than its share of teenage suicides. Like most towns in South Wales, it suffered economically as the coal mines closed, but recovered more quickly than some, with job opportunities opening up as multi-nationals moved in.

Is Suicide Catching?

But then, there is often no obvious reason for the suicide clusters which have cropped up from time to time throughout history. Researchers have long acknowledged that suicide can be "catching", with those who have lost a loved one in this way more at risk of taking their own life.

Sigmund Freud held a conference on the phenomenon in the 1920s, researcher David Phillips christened it "the Werther effect" after Goethe's book, *The Sorrows Of Young Werther*, which is said to have inspired several young men to shoot themselves in the 18th century, and sociologist Loren Coleman wrote a book on it in the late 1980s.

In the last six months alone [August 2007–February 2008], two distraught mothers have committed suicide months after their teenage daughters killed themselves. Suicide clusters are also common in closed communities such as prisons, psychiatric hospitals, military barracks or schools, or in small towns where people are more likely to know each other. Four friends in Cromarty, in the Black Isle, killed themselves within the space of 12 months in 2004–05.

What is less clear is what lies behind such clusters. Dr Stephen Platt, of Edinburgh University's Research Unit in Health and Behavioural Change, says research suggests a large number of factors have to combine in specific circumstances for a spate of copycat suicides to occur. Underlying social problems, the way people interact and the poor mental health of those involved may all play a part.

"There is certainly evidence [that] the risk of imitative behaviour after a suicide can be affected by the community response to it—if suicide is romanticised or normalised in any way it can lead to imitative behaviour," says Platt. "Studies of non-fatal suicidal behaviour (self-harming), initiatives that allow the victim to gain either extra attention or services by their action has increased rather than decreased the problem."

Shortly after Bonnie McClelland's son Timothy killed himself, two of his friends followed suit. "As a parent, your heart is already shattered. But then, to look into the eyes of your friends and see the pain that your child has caused, is something you carry in your heart forever," McClelland, who lives in Tampa, Florida, said.

Suicide as Solution

In the year following Timothy's death there were 29 teenage suicides in her local area. "When a suicide happens, it's like a book has been taken off the library shelf. They open that book and it gives them the direction of what to do."

The 16 young people who killed themselves in Bridgend came from very different backgrounds. Eighteen-year-old Dale Crole, the first suicide victim, had recently been freed from a young offenders' institution and lived with his father, with whom he was said to have a volatile relationship.

Zachary Barnes, 17, had left school to work on the Amelia Trust Farm near Barry, but hoped to become a fitness instructor. Natasha Randall, also 17, who used the name sxiwildchild, studied care and childhood studies at Bridgend College.

What united them, beyond individual friendships, was that they all came to see suicide as a viable solution to whatever difficulties they were experiencing.

With no evidence whatsoever that these youngsters encouraged each other to commit suicide, it would be irresponsible to refer to their deaths as a pact or a cult. The personal circumstances of those involved are too disparate—and the links between them too tenuous even to refer to them as an epidemic.

Yet, it is clear from the Bebo messages sent in the wake of every tragedy—many of which could be seen as normalising or glamorising suicide—how the self-inflicted deaths have impacted on the entire community.

There can now be few young people in Bridgend who do not know someone who knows someone who has died; and few parents who are not frantically worried about their own teenage children's emotional well-being.

It is easy to see how mounting publicity and hysteria could leave the vulnerable at greater risk of following suit. Yet, those closest to the tragedy—from parents to politicians—seem at a loss as to what is happening or how to stop it. "It's like a craze—a stupid sort of fad. They all seem to be copying each other by wanting to die," said Melanie Davies, whose son Thomas killed himself following the deaths of his friends, Dale and David.

Claustrophobia

MP Madeleine Moon puts some of Bridgend's plight down to the insular nature of the community. "In all honesty, Bridgend is not socially deprived," she has said. "Perhaps one of the problems is young people need to raise their levels of aspiration. I've got two towns and lots of villages (in my constituency]. They are very close communities in which everyone knows everyone else. People don't like to move 500 yards to the next village because their whole identity is around the village their families grew up in.

"But there is a downside. I was speaking to a group of girls recently and they were saying it could be claustrophobic. Everything that happens to you, everyone else knows about it, so it can be harder to deal with. You feel much more exposed. So, if you have a relationship breakup it's the gossip of the village. So there is pressure there."

Although there is unease at the way teenagers in Bridgend used the internet to read about and comment on the suicides, most people seem to believe it is a scapegoat for more complex problems and a longstanding failure to tackle them. "I believe there is a risk from spending too much time in the alternative reality of computer games and chat rooms. I also be-

Teenage girl contemplating suicide. Image copyright @erics, 2009. Used under license from Shutterstock.com.

lieve that, for a vulnerable person who is contemplating suicide, the isolation of communication through words on a screen does not provide the warmth, humanity, compassion and empathy of talking to another person," admits Moon.

But the MP is more concerned that despite its high suicide rate, Wales does not have a Suicide Prevention Strategy similar to those introduced in Scotland and England.

While she waits for funding, Bridgend braces itself for more tragedy. On Friday [February 15, 2008], a girl called Rosie, who claims to know seven of the victims, posted a message on Stephenson's website which seemed to sum up the punch-drunk community's sense of bewilderment.

"It's going crazy (here) and it's not going to stop," she said. "No one can understand what is going on. People are saying it's got something to do with the internet, but I don't believe that. But then I can't explain it either."

Teenage Violence

Janell Ross and Christian Bottorff

Janell Ross is a staff writer for the Nashville Tennessean, *and Christian Bottorff was a police reporter for the same paper.*

Teenage violence is a perpetual problem in the twenty-first-century United States, when "bodies outpace brains," as reported in the following article by Janell Ross and Christian Bottorff. By October 15, 2007, fourteen juveniles had been charged in ten of Nashville, Tennessee's killings throughout the year. In Nashville, the vast majority of teenage killings are gang related. Like the patriarchy in Romeo and Juliet, *the parents of young killers bear immense responsibility for their children's behavior. Parents tear their families apart, keep arms in their homes where children can have access to them, and, in general, do not provide them with good role models. Children, sometimes abandoned, receive inadequate attention, much less guidance. The conclusion reached by many in Nashville is that the answer does not lie in more law enforcement and prisons, but in getting to the root of the problem.*

Teenagers have been charged in 10 of Nashville's 51 killings this year [2007]. All but one of the cases involved a handgun. One started as an argument between two teens over household chores. Another started with an attempt to rob people chatting on a front porch. Each time, the end result was the same. Someone wound up dead, and a juvenile—a child 17 or younger—was charged with homicide. This year, 14 juveniles have been charged in 10 of Nashville's 51 killings.

Teen Violence in Nashville

On Oct. 8, a 14-year-old Nashville boy shot and killed Classie Wilson, a beloved 70-year-old market owner inside her east Nashville store, police said. That shooting is bringing several patterns into focus. Most of the youth suspects—12 of them—are African-American teenage males. And all but one of the cases involved a handgun. Those patterns are raising questions about how young African-American males are getting guns, why so many allegedly have been involved in homicides this year, and what is being done to reverse the deadly trends.

Cities the size of Nashville usually see 10 percent to 12 percent of homicides committed by juvenile offenders, said Gary Jensen, a criminologist at Vanderbilt University who specializes in issues related to juvenile and violent crime. But in Nashville this year, juveniles are responsible for nearly 20 percent of Nashville's homicides, according to police. "That is unusual," Jensen said. "That seems quite high." What's happening with African-American teenage males in Nashville is happening in other cities, said Marino Bruce, a Meharry Medical College associate professor who studies the social and psychological factors linked to risky behavior. But he cautioned against attributing their criminality to race, or simply saying that it's the result of parenting, schools or any lone cause. "It's a complex issue," Bruce said. "We have a tendency to oversimplify because it simplifies us. Pardon the pun, but we want a magic bullet. But when you're dealing with human behavior it's never that simple."

Lack of Role Models

Nevertheless, the past few weeks have seen an explosion of violence among juveniles in Nashville, much of it fueled by robberies, said Jeff Burks, an assistant district attorney who handles juvenile cases. "It's never about the money," Burks said. "It's about being in the gang, proving yourself to the gang or 'I'm bad.' "Other leaders expressed concern about how some teens define manly behavior. The Rev. Ronnie Mitchell, pastor at New Livingstone Baptist Church in east Nashville, sees many teens who don't have fathers in the home having their worldviews shaped by entertainers, athletes and violent video games.

The Bailey Middle student who is charged with shooting the store owner apparently got the gun from his aunt's home, where he lived after he was removed from his parents' custody. Steve Scruggs, the aunt's longtime boyfriend and the man who served as the teen's surrogate father, said the family had the gun for protection. "We live out east, and you never know what's going to happen out here," Scruggs said. Last week [October 2007], in the living room at the home he shared with the teen and his aunt, Scruggs showed a reporter another gun he kept buried between sofa cushions for easy access. It's a home where framed pictures of the alleged teen gunman as a toddler line the walls, and a home that is a mile from the Cahal Avenue market where the owner was killed.

An open-air drug market and a thriving prostitution trade operate a few blocks away from the rapidly gentrifying neighborhood, Scruggs said. The area Scruggs referred to was for many years a known drug market, said East Precinct Sgt. Michael Dioguardi. But police are no longer frequently called to the area, he said. "You have to be ready for robberies, home invasions, somebody trying to come in here," Scruggs said. Scruggs said he had no idea that the teen was interested in guns or was aggressive enough to attempt a robbery, much less shoot a gun.

Bodies Outpace Brains

Aggressive behavior among teenagers is not uncommon. Today, teens are physically maturing faster than they were 20 to 30 years ago and are exposed to mature ideas earlier in their lives, according to Julia Graber, an associate professor at the University of Florida in Gainesville who studies brain development in teens. Graber said that teens' brains aren't developing as quickly as their bodies. The frontal lobe—the part of the brain that helps control impulses, analyze and organize information and connect action to long-term consequence—develops over the teen years. In most people, it's not complete until their early 20s. Eva Steele, a mother of seven, thought she understood children. But in May, she saw a 14-year-old boy shoot and kill her 22-year-old nephew Chauncey Shelton while Shelton was breaking up a fight between two groups of girls. "It's like they don't have any conscience," Steele said. "They do things and either don't feel bad about them or don't realize how bad they are." That still doesn't explain why so many of the teens charged with homicide are African-American.

Economics and Environment

"It's economics, the environment and just hopelessness," said the Rev. James Turner II, a youth pastor at New Hope Baptist Church who heads the African American Male Risk Reduction Committee for the Nashville Prevention Partnership. "When you look up, you can't get a job, and you see other black males who can't get a job. You say, 'What am I to do?' The violence—you can't get in a child's mind to see what pushed them. It's not gang related. That is just the individual. That child has to explain why he did what he did. But with poor black males, we have been hit so many ways. You see black males dying. It's survival."

The leading indicators that a person is likely to be involved in violent crimes are unemployment levels in their communities and family, poverty, being raised in a single parent home, communities with high dropout rates, living in an urban setting, and the availability of guns, said Jensen, the Vanderbilt criminologist. These also are issues that disproportionately affect African-American families. For example, the overall unemployment rate in Tennessee [in 2006] was just over 5 percent, but the unemployment rate for African-American workers was 10.3 percent. The rate is based on workers who are actively seeking jobs.

Pastors from several predominantly African-American Nashville churches in communities where some of these problems are prevalent said Nashville has reached a critical point. There are communities that foster social ills such as hunger, addiction and in some cases a lack of parental concern, said Mitchell, New Livingstone's pastor. Mitchell pointed to the disproportionately high number of African-American men who are and have been in prison and unavailable to be parents. As a result, the cycle continues. Schools, churches and mentoring programs are left to fill the void, said the Rev. Enoch Fuzz, pastor at Corinthian Baptist Church in north Nashville. "Poverty is the enemy of the law," Fuzz said.

Parents' Responsibility

The Tennessean tried to gather details about the home lives, school attendance and criminal histories of all 14 juveniles charged with homicide this year. The state Department of Children's Services never had contact with eight of the teens, a spokesman said. Officials declined to comment about the other six. Tennessee law bars them from discussing details about children in state custody. The Metro school district would provide no details about the teens' attendance, citing a federal education privacy law. Metro police say there are no simple answers for what is causing the teen violence or what they can do to stop it.

Violent juvenile crime has spiked this year by 92 percent, Metro police records show. Police said 11 juveniles were arrested on homicide charges last year, and only five were charged with homicide in 2005. "If there was one silver bullet that could fix it, wouldn't we use it?" Metro Police Chief Ronal Serpas said in an interview. "But that's not available to us . . . it's going to take a whole community to deal with this issue."

Police and prosecutors plan to begin charging parents and guardians with contributing to the delinquency of a minor when their influence and behavior are to blame for a child's actions, Serpas said. He also pointed to school dropout rates as a factor.

In 2005, about 62 percent of Metro public school students graduated from high school on time. Last year, that number grew to nearly 69 percent but fell short of the state's 90 percent on-time graduation goal. In the 2005–06 school year, the most recent with data available, 67.3 percent of African-American students graduated on time, compared with 68.5 percent of all students.

"Truancy is parallel to learning, and we are certainly learning that it is parallel to safety," said Ralph Thompson, assistant superintendent for student services. The district is operating programs to improve student behavior, provide counseling to students and help kids with poor attendance catch up, Thompson said.

Serpas said that since early 2006, he has assigned two detectives full time to visit parents of troubled children. Since the program started, the detectives have gone into at least 1,000 homes, handing out pamphlets about social service agencies that can help them. Mitchell, the New Livingstone pastor, said that in 2005 Serpas and then-Mayor Bill Purcell were seeking ideas to curb youth violence and black-on-black crime. Murders had climbed that year to 100, a near record. Half of those killed, and those arrested, were young African-American males. A group of African-American clergymen said they would create programs to train African-American males as skilled tradesmen if the mayor and Serpas could ensure the workers would be hired to build publicly funded projects.

The training programs were put together and continue today, but the jobs never materialized, the clergymen said. Serpas said, through a police department spokesman, that he was not aware of the plan. Newly elected Mayor Karl Dean, who campaigned on creating solutions to address youth crime, pledged that the city would focus on "stepped-up law enforcement" in the short term and cut into the Metro school district's dropout rate in the long term. "What I've talked about is the need to have a combined emphasis on law enforcement and tough prosecution with, obviously, making efforts to keep kids in school," Dean said.

The Root of the Problem

Prosecutors want all 14 juveniles charged with homicide to be tried as adults. A judge has already decided that eight of them should go to adult court, and decisions on the others are pending. Prosecutors haven't decided how to prosecute the teen accused of killing Cahal Street merchant Classie Wilson. "We're going to look into his past, and we're going to have to evaluate the facts of this particular case," said Tony Johnson, the Davidson County district attorney. Howard Gentry, former Nashville vice mayor, said Nashville has reached the point where the problems affecting African-American teenagers cannot be ignored. "You are not going to be able to hire enough police, you are not going to be able to build enough prisons to handle and house them all," said Gentry, leader of a Nashville Chamber of Commerce foundation that addresses public safety. "That is why it is critical . . . that we address the root causes, the things that are leading some boys down this path."

Turner, the youth pastor, said leaders—particularly African-American politicians, clergymen and Nashville business owners—must get involved in resolving some portion of the problem. "Black leaders, political officers, those who are council members, all those, any black organizations have got to step up to the plate," Turner said. "The young say the black leadership in Nashville, Tennessee, has not stepped up to the plate to fight for them."

Youth Violence Around the World

Edmund Sanders

Edmund Sanders is a staff writer for the Los Angeles Times.

As remote as sixteenth-century Verona is in time and place from twenty-first-century Africa, stories of youthful violence in places such as the African nation of Kenya have much in common with violence in Romeo and Juliet. *As Edmund Sanders explain in the following viewpoint, youthful violence knows no national boundaries. Much of the fighting springs from tribal feuds, similar to gangs around the world. It arises from youthful discontent with the older generation and its corrupt patriarchy that rules with an iron hand. Despite the tribal divide, couples from different tribes have married. Bernard, a young Kenyan man, for example, runs with a gang that randomly kills with machetes and torches homes and businesses, but he consistently quotes the Bible and is fanatically against the drinking of alcohol. He rages against the Kikuyu tribe, but has chosen a young Kikuyu woman for his girlfriend. Bernard is similar to the males in Shakespeare's Verona in that much of the physical violence he perpetrates and experiences has inner parallels in moral contradictions and internal strife.*

He's a preacher's son and part-time college student who idolizes Martin Luther King Jr. and aspires to escape Kenya's biggest slum.

But when this East African nation erupted in postelection chaos, an unfamiliar rage took over inside the boyish-looking 21-year-old.

Rivalry and Violence

"I felt like my life had been stolen," said Bernard, whose last name was withheld for his protection. "In my mind, I wanted to damage everything. I picked up a *rungu* [wooden club] and started to run."

Bernard has joined hundreds of other opposition supporters in looting shops of sugar, flour and cellphones. He doused businesses owned by rival tribes with gasoline and set them afire. During one fateful attack, he grabbed a machete and roamed the slums with a mob hellbent on finding someone to kill.

Angry young men such as Bernard are at the heart of Kenya's descent into violence and destruction. But just how a Bible-quoting fellow like Bernard can be transformed into a stone-throwing rioter has mystified many, both in- and outside Kenya.

Twenty-something Kenyans are more educated, ethnically integrated and exposed to such democratic ideals as human rights and freedom than previous generations. Yet they've reacted more violently, tribally and defiantly than their parents could ever imagine doing.

Coming of age at a time when Kenya is in political and economic transition, young people here have one foot in a modern, Westernized ideal of what their country might become and another rooted in African traditions and history.

"It's harder for this generation," Bernard's father said. "They have so many more choices and decisions."

A Jumble of Moral Contradictions

It's small wonder that Bernard can seem a jumble of moral contradictions. He laughs off looting as harmless "shopping," but shuns alcohol because he says it violates his religious ethics. He's of the opposition Luo tribe and dates a girl of the rival Kikuyu tribe, yet calls Kikuyus "thieves" and betrayed a former high school friend to Luo gangs, who later beat up the youth and burned his house.

His toughest choice came [in January 2008] when a gang of enraged youths from his neighborhood asked him to join their revenge squad to kill the first Kikuyu they found. Heart racing, Bernard hesitated for a moment.

"Part of me didn't want to go," he said. "I was afraid of what might happen. But I grabbed my panga [machete] and followed."

Minutes later he would learn just how deep this newfound anger ran.

Bernard's story is just one piece of the puzzle that might explain why Kenya has turned so quickly from an African role model into a cautionary tale. What began as frustration over the disputed Dec. 27 [2007] presidential election has uncorked long-standing tensions over ethnicity, poverty, and competition for land and power.

Feuds, Poverty, and Violence

Much of the anger has been directed at President Mwai Kibaki's Kikuyu tribe, which has dominated Kenyan politics since independence and enjoyed the fruits of economic expansion. Luos accuse Kikuyus of hoarding money and power. They'd hoped the election of opposition leader Raila Odinga, a Luo, would bring them power, jobs and economic opportunity.

Those hopes collapsed when Kibaki was declared the winner, despite allegations of vote rigging and other election irregularities. Now Kenya's economy is in tatters, the nation's reputation for democratic progress stained.

Bernard's story begins in Kibera, a notorious Nairobi slum populated largely by Luos. Built along a colonial-era railroad line, the impoverished area of the capital counts nearly 1 million people crammed on hilly land.

His family is divided for economic reasons. He lives with his father, a pastor who works as a government clerk, and a sister. For more than a decade, his mother has lived in western Kenya, taking care of four other siblings in school there.

Bernard has enjoyed educational opportunities his parents never had. His father dropped out of high school to help support his family; Bernard attends college part time.

Yet life in the slum is dismal, he said. Lack of toilets means streams of sewage run through dirt trenches and fecal dust in the air causes frequent infections. Crime and muggings are common. Most people are unemployed.

Though Kenya's economy surged 7% [in 2007], there's little evidence of prosperity in Kibera. Fueling ethnic resentment is the fact that most of the shops and homes are owned by Kikuyus.

"They grow up bitter here," said Pastor Andrew Ouma of the African Inland Church. "And a poor man usually thinks he's poor because of the rich man."

Bernard is studying to be a journalist, but remains pessimistic about his job prospects.

"People here have lost hope," he said. "But you can't survive without hope. I'd rather live without food than live without hope."

Much of Kibera's outburst can be attributed to rebellion against long-standing poverty and economic marginalization, experts say.

Revolt Against the Older Generation

"It boils down to their frustration," said Ken Ouko, a sociologist at the University of Nairobi who specializes in youth. He says recent unrest also has been fueled by classic youthful revolt against the older generation, noting that Kenya's political leaders are in their 60s and 70s.

The flawed election was a trigger, Ouko says, providing young people with an outlet to vent their anger as well as a cause to rally around. He noted that young rioters in Kibera and elsewhere have been seen smiling and laughing, even as police fired tear gas and bullets.

"Half the time they look like they are enjoying themselves," Ouko said. "This conflict in a way is giving a meaning to their lives."

Young people say their higher education and greater awareness have made them more vehement and desperate, not less. Increased access to satellite television, the internet, e-mail and cellphones during the last five years has made young Kenyans acutely aware of their standing in the world.

"Young people today understand their rights," said Teresa Mutegi, deputy principal at Langata Secondary School, which draws 90% of its students from Kibera. "They see the rest of the world. That's why they are more aggressive and more ambitious. They are saying, 'Give us what is ours.'". . .

Ironically, many of the freedoms young people now enjoy were delivered by the man they vilify, Kibaki, who expanded free speech and the rights of a free press and made primary education free. Before Kibaki began his first term at the end of 2002, openly criticizing the head of state was unthinkable and government opponents found themselves in secret torture chambers.

Liz, 23, who works as a day laborer in Kibera, said young people are reacting so fiercely because they fear Kibaki is trying to reverse the rights he expanded by "stealing" the election. "Yes, Kibaki gave us the freedoms, but in the last minute he took them away," she said. "He opened the window and now is trying to close it."

Without question, the surge in tribalism among young people has been the most shocking twist to the current violence. The young generation is the most ethnically integrated, thanks to urbanization and increased mobility. For years, different tribes lived side by side without problems. Intermarriage was common.

A youth pleads for his safety as he is attacked by other youth from the opposition supporters during post-election violence in Nairobi, Kenya on January 23, 2008. AP Images.

An Internal Tug-of-War

But tribal rivalry has resurfaced with a vengeance in young people, who led many of the ethnically targeted killings and village burnings.

Young people might be reaching back to their tribal roots as a last resort, sociologist Ouko explained, believing that support systems, including government, church and family, have failed to address their plight. "There's an institutional collapse," Ouko said. "So they are looking for a Plan B. They are beginning to internalize tribe."

The internal tug-of-war is apparent in Bernard. One minute he condemned tribal killings, and said he saw no reason to break up with his Kikuyu girlfriend. In the next breath, he said that in light of the recent fighting, tribes should live in segregated neighborhoods. And he spoke with cold detachment of the recent killing of a Kikuyu doctor beheaded by gangs. "If we can't kill Kibaki, the next best thing is kill the Kikuyu neighbors," he said.

Such competing emotions were in play Jan. 29 [2008] when the gang arrived at his door to recruit him. A Luo member of parliament had just been assassinated. "'Come with us,'" he said they told him. "'We're going to kill a Kikuyu.'"

Bernard described previous looting and burning attacks as "fun," but he joined reluctantly this time, he said.

Growing up in Kibera, he had seen corpses many times, usually victims of street crime. But he'd never watched a man die. When the gang descended upon its Kikuyu victim, Bernard said, he stood frozen on the sidelines, watching the blood gush from the victim's neck and head.

In that moment, rage gave way to another emotion: pity.

"I felt such regret," he said. "Suddenly I saw life as this game, where you have it one second and it's gone the next. People don't respect it. It touched me."

Bernard slipped away from the gang, he said, and returned home, stowing his panga and not telling his father.

Afterward, Bernard said his anger subsided. He doubted that he would take part again in protests and was hoping school would reopen so he could resume his studies. Kibera, he hoped, would stay quiet.

Then early [in February 2008], his father was laid off. The family blames tribal discrimination. The supervisor is a Kikuyu and the suspended workers Luos.

Bernard rested his head in one hand. He's worried about how the family will pay for food and his school fees.

"Now," he said quietly, "the hatred is coming again."

For Further Discussion

1. Discuss, or perhaps stage a debate around, the conflicting facts about Shakespeare's own marriage. What details seem to support that he was in a forced and loveless marriage? What details suggest that it was an enduring marriage of love? Cite from the essays by John F. Andrews and Peter Ackroyd in your discussion/debate.

2. Debate the question of whether the younger Juliet matures before Romeo does, citing from the essays by Marjorie Garber and Cedric Watts.

3. How does rebellion against social traditions and, especially against parents, become a necessary part of growing up in *Romeo and Juliet*? Does such rebellion remain inevitable? Cite from the essays by Robert Appelbaum and Sharon Hamilton in your answers.

4. How does the sense of honor and its consequent violence in the society of Shakespeare's Verona impede maturity— not only that of its children but its patriarchs? In your answers cite from the essays by Jill L. Levenson and Dympna Callaghan.

5. Discuss the parallel tragedies of growing up, as portrayed by the story of Romeo and Juliet, with maturing in the twenty-first century, using information from the articles by Dani Garavelli, Stephen Singular, Katherine Gazella, Janell Ross and Christian Bottorff in your answer.

For Further Reading

Robert Burton, *The Anatomy of Melancholy*. Oxford: Clarendon Press, 1989.

Thomas Dekker, *The Shoemaker's Holiday*. Manchester: Manchester University Press, 1979.

John Ford, *'Tis Pity She's a Whore*, in *The Selected Plays of John Ford*. Ed. Colin Gibson. Cambridge: Cambridge University Press, 1986.

Thomas Heywood, *A Woman Killed with Kindness*, in *Three Elizabethan Domestic Tragedies*. Ed. Keith Sturgess. New York: Penguin, 1985.

Ben Jonson, *Volpone*. Ed. Brian Parker and David Bevington. New York: St. Martin's, 1999.

Thomas Middleton, *The Changeling*. New York: Norton, 2006.

William Shakespeare, *All's Well That Ends Well*, in *The Riverside Shakespeare*. Boston: Houghton Mifflin, 1974.

———, *Love's Labours Lost*, in *The Riverside Shakespeare*. Boston: Houghton Mifflin, 1974.

———, *Measure for Measure*, in *The Riverside Shakespeare*. Boston: Houghton Mifflin, 1974.

———, *A Midsummer Night's Dream*, in *The Riverside Shakespeare*. Boston: Houghton Mifflin, 1974.

———, *Much Ado About Nothing*, in *The Riverside Shakespeare*. Boston: Houghton Mifflin, 1974.

———, *Sonnets*, in *The Riverside Shakespeare*. Boston: Houghton Mifflin, 1974.

———, *The Taming of the Shrew*, in *The Riverside Shakespeare*. Boston: Houghton Mifflin, 1974.

———, *The Tempest*, in *The Riverside Shakespeare*. Boston: Houghton Mifflin, 1974.

———, *Troilus and Cressida*, in *The Riverside Shakespeare*. Boston: Houghton Mifflin, 1974.

Philip Sidney, *Astrophel and Stella*. Ed. Mona Wilson. London: Nonesuch, 1931.

John Webster, *The Duchess of Malfi*. Bristol, UK: Bristol Classical Publications, 1989.

Bibliography

Books

Ian W. Archer	*The Pursuit of Stability: Social Relations in Elizabethan London.* Cambridge: Cambridge University Press, 1991.
Jeffrey Jensen Arnett	*Adolescence and Emerging Adulthood.* Upper Saddle River, NJ: Pearson/Prentice-Hall, 2007.
Kathleen Stassen Berger	*The Developing Person Through Childhood and Adolescence.* New York: Worth, 2000.
Maurice Charney	*Shakespeare on Love and Lust.* New York: Columbia University Press, 2000.
Ann Jenalie Cook	*Making a Match: Courtship in Shakespeare and His Society.* Princeton, NJ: Princeton University Press, 1991.
Katherine Dalsimer	"Middle Adolescence: *Romeo and Juliet*," in *Female Adolescence: Psychoanalytic Reflections on Works of Literature.* New Haven, CT: Yale University Press, 1986.
Irene G. Dash	*Wooing Wedding, and Power.* New York: Columbia University Press, 1981.

Diane E. Dreher   *Domination and Defiance: Fathers and Daughters in Shakespeare.* Lexington: University Press of Kentucky, 1985.

Kirby Farrell   "Love, Death, and Patriarchy," in *Play, Death, and Heroism in Shakespeare.* Chapel Hill: University of North Carolina Press, 1989.

Marjorie Garber   *Coming of Age in Shakespeare.* London: Methuen, 1981.

Laura Gowing   *Domestic Dangers: Women, Words and Sex in Early Modern London.* Oxford: Clarendon Press, 1998.

Alice Griffin, ed.   *Rebels and Lovers: Shakespeare's Young Heroes and Heroines.* New York: New York University Press, 1976.

Lisa Hopkins   *The Shakespearean Marriage.* New York: Macmillan, 1998.

Jerry Jacobs   *Adolescent Suicide.* New York: Wiley, 1971.

Robert A. King and Alan Apter   *Suicide in Children and Adolescents.* Cambridge: Cambridge University Press, 2003.

Arthur C. Kirsch   *Shakespeare's Apprenticeship.* Chicago: University of Chicago Press, 1974.

William G. Meader   *Courtship in Shakespeare.* New York: King's Crown, 1954.

| Rolf E. Muuss, ed. | *Adolescent Behavior and Society: A Book of Readings.* New York: McGraw Hill, 1990. |

| Charles Nicholl | *The Lodger Shakespeare: His Life on Silver Street.* New York: Viking, 2008. |

| M.M. Reese | *Shakespeare: His World and His Work.* London: Arnold, 1953. |

| Sylvia Rimm | *Growing Up Too Fast.* Emmaus, PA: Rodale, 2005. |

| A.L. Rowse | *William Shakespeare: A Biography.* London: Macmillan, 1965. |

| Samuel Schuenbaum | *William Shakespeare: A Documentary Life.* New York: Oxford University Press, 1975. |

| Reva Seth | *First Comes Marriage: Modern Relationship Advice from the Wisdom of Arranged Marriages.* New York: Simon and Schuster, 2008. |

| Franklin E. Zimring | *American Youth Violence.* New York: Oxford University Press, 1998. |

Periodicals

| Lynda Boose | "The Father and the Bride in Shakespeare," *PMLA*, vol. 97, 1982. |

| Marjorie Cox | "Adolescent Processes in *Romeo and Juliet*," *Psychoanalytic Review*, vol. 63, 1976. |

Lloyd Davis	"Desire and Presence in *Romeo and Juliet*," *Shakespeare Survey*, vol. 49, 1996.
Phyllis L. Ellickson et al.	"Adolescence: Forgotten Ages, Forgotten Problems," *Rand Research Review*, Spring 1997.
M.D. Faber	"The Adolescent Suicides of *Romeo and Juliet*," *Psychoanalytic Review*, vol. 59, 1972–1973.
J. Karl Franson	"Too Soon Marr'd: Juliet's Age as Symbol in *Romeo and Juliet*," *Papers on Language and Literature*, vol. 32, 1996.
S.F. Lambert, N.S. Ialongo, R.C. Boyd, and M.R. Cooley	"Risk Factors for Community Violence Exposure Adolescence," *American Journal of Community Psychology*, September 2005.
Paul N. Siegel	"Christianity and the Religion of Love in *Romeo and Juliet*," *Shakespeare Quarterly*, vol. 12, 1961.
Susan Snyder	"Ideology and Feud in *Romeo and Juliet*," *Shakespeare Survey*, vol. 49, 1996.
Robin Wells	"Neo-Petrarchian Kitsch in *Romeo and Juliet*," *Modern Language Review*, October 1998.

Internet Sources

Duncan Greenberg	"Students Have Always Been Violent," *Slate*, May 7, 1999. www.slate.com.

Index